THE UNIVERSITY of ROCHESTER PRESS

THE UNIVERSITY *of* ROCHESTER PRESS

A Brief History of the First Twenty Years

Brian J. Thompson

UNIVERSITY OF ROCHESTER PRESS

First published 2009
University of Rochester Press
668 Mt. Hope Avenue, Rochester, NY 14620, USA
www.urpress.com
and Boydell & Brewer Limited
PO Box 9, Woodbridge, Suffolk IP12 3DF, UK
www.boydellandbrewer.com

Thompson, Brian J.
The University of Rochester Press : a brief history of the first twenty years / Brian J. Thompson.
    p. cm.
Includes bibliographical references.
ISBN 978-1-58046-360-7 (pbk. : alk. paper) 1. University of Rochester Press—History. 2. University presses—New York (State)—Rochester—History. 3. Scholarly publishing—New York (State)—Rochester—History. 4. University of Rochester Press—Bibliography. 5. Rochester (N.Y.)—Imprints. I. Title.
Z473.U67T48   2009
070.5'94–dc22

2009044956

This publication is printed on acid-free paper.
Printed in the United States of America.

This volume is dedicated to the memory of Professor Derek Brewer, preeminent scholar of medieval literature, founder of the publishing imprint D. S. Brewer, and Master of Emmanuel College, Cambridge. Professor Brewer was instrumental in the formation of the University of Rochester Press in partnership with Boydell & Brewer Ltd. He was an outstanding academic colleague and friend and served on the Editorial Board of the University of Rochester Press for many years.

✆ CONTENTS

Foreword by Ralph W. Kuncl   ix

Acknowledgments   xiii

  1   A Press for the University   1

  2   The Agreement   8

  3   The Press Is Launched   15

  4   The List through the Years   30

  5   The Serious Business of Scholarly Series   51

  6   Meliora: An Imprint for the University   87

  7   Cooperative Ventures   92

  8   Looking Forward   98

Appendix   103

✑ FOREWORD

A MODEL OF ITS KIND

RALPH W. KUNCL, PROVOST AND EXECUTIVE VICE
PRESIDENT, UNIVERSITY OF ROCHESTER

THERE IS SOMETHING ABOUT TURNING TWENTY. A twentieth anniversary—whether of a business, a marriage, or a school graduation—presents an opportunity to take stock of oneself, one's impact, one's place among peers. This volume does just that, assessing the University of Rochester Press through history and analysis. What we see is impressive. Our impact on young scholars seeking their way, our impact on the fields of music, culture, and history, and our business practices are all models of their kind. Further, in changing times, when digital media challenge the nature of newspapers, research libraries, and book reading, the Press finds itself thriving, not in the dire circumstances of some more traditionally structured presses.

One feature of the landscape of scholarship on which I live as a chief academic officer is the growing financial concern of many university presses. Most of them require subsidization by the host university, sometimes to the extent of many hundreds of thousands or even millions of dollars per year. Some presses have severely declined; others have found refuge in consortia to control the fixed costs of printing, warehousing, marketing, and distribution. A 2009 survey of the members of the Association of American University Presses reported that in 2005–8 all size categories of presses had average net operating expenses that exceeded income. Three-fourths required subvention from their parent institutions, totaling $25.2 million in 2008 for the fifty presses that reported subsidies—an average per press of over a half million dollars! That does not even account for the vast in-kind support from the parent institution that is typical of university presses. Further surveys showed a decline in net sales in 2008–9 of 10–12 percent, worse in the smaller presses, and those figures predate the great economic global recession that peaked in early 2009. It paints a troubling picture. When I came to the University of Rochester, therefore, I was surprised and intrigued by the configuration of the UR Press, a press that was, by "intelligent design," *not* to rely on significant institutional subsidy but rather to make its *own* way.

A second (and also troubling) attribute of scholarly publishing nowadays is the seemingly inexorable decline in publishing venues for first-book authors in the humanities and humanistic social sciences. That fact threatens the pipeline of future faculty and prompts many of us to offer subventions to young faculty who are navigating the challenge of getting their first books published by a prestigious press with a reputation for strong editorial practices and critical peer review. The UR Press offers guidance to early-career university faculty and solicits and publishes their exceptional work in select fields; this has been altruistic, to be sure, but it has also opened a new stream of authors and ideas. I expect that subventions for young authors will need to continue. Indeed, with eroding revenues for publishing it seems likely that the academy may need to underwrite more vigorously the publications of its established scholars as well, unless the digital revolution solves that problem by creating new markets for scholarship.

In this rocky economic and scholarly landscape in higher education, the UR Press is a model of innovation. Several key editorial and business practices have sustained it and will continue to let it thrive.

Guided first by a philosophy of selective editorial excellence, we don't attempt to "cover a field" in any of our series. Instead, our editors carefully assess the intellectual interest for each title. As a result, the Press over the years has established critical prestige in such areas as musicology, African studies, medical history, and early modern European history. Attention to interdisciplinarity (for example, ethnomusicology) is also a path not only to excellent scholarship but marketability.

A second philosophy is that good business sense accompanies editorial acumen. The emphasis on careful series editorship, topical focus, and title choices is matched by careful attention to costs of production and sustainable pricing. Business sense also extends to many key traits, including the careful, nonformulaic determination of press runs. Nimbleness is evidenced by moving immediately to print-on-demand when an initial modest run is sold out or when classic imprints remain indefinitely in demand.

Finally, the UR Press thrives because, from the beginning, it has forged collaborations. Uniquely tapping into the knowledge of a savvy partner, Boydell & Brewer Ltd., was a strategic move. Sharing costs of production and marketing was key to getting the Press off the ground. On a continuing basis, the simultaneous promotion and distribution of new titles from the U.S. and U.K. offices not only constrains mailing costs but greatly benefits authors, whose works are promoted, sold, and distributed internationally from the first print run. But the even more distinctive characteristics of the partner—an independent, privately-owned, for-profit publisher that was scholarly in its own right—assured the shared motivations essential to a compatible alliance. The Press also celebrates the art of the book through its collegial relationship with one of the most innovative research university libraries in the U.S.: the University of Rochester River Campus Libraries, including Rush Rhees Library, where most recently an anthropological, student-centered approach to modern library design has drawn national attention.

Still, despite the strength and nimbleness of the UR Press, uncertain times are ahead: the ever more complex and difficult economy we perhaps may come to call the "new normal," and the uncertain but vastly new and still emergent methods of publication. How will the business model for open access publishing or any digital-only publishing really work? As the twentieth-year history now in your hands tells, UR Press has been innovative and flexible from its very start. I have no doubt it is well positioned to adapt and to continue adding to the valuable scholarship being produced by faculty around the world.

⁓ ACKNOWLEDGMENTS

THE AUTHOR GRATEFULLY ACKNOWLEDGES the contributions herein from series editors Theodore M. Brown, Jim Collins, Toyin Falola, and Ralph P. Locke, as well as the considerable efforts of University of Rochester Press editorial director Suzanne E. Guiod and editorial board chair Robert Kraus in bringing this manuscript to its final form.

chapter 1

A PRESS FOR THE UNIVERSITY

The University of Rochester has historically prided itself on being focused—never seeking to be all things to all people, but rather concentrating on those things it could do very well. In fact, some of the programs developed across the disciplines typical of a research university set the model for similar efforts now seen at other institutions. The University has contributed generously to the world of scholarship, to the education of generations of students, and to the institution's local community.

It comes as no surprise, then, that the University of Rochester Press, now in its twentieth year, has made its mark using a selective approach. From its inception, the Press has maintained a focus on select areas of scholarship as a way of defining its niche in academic publishing. A small university press producing approximately twenty-five new titles each year, URP continues to bring notable scholarship in these areas to the larger academic world, even as it adjusts to the changing fortunes of scholarly publishing. And, like so many of the University of Rochester's intellectual accomplishments over the years, the Press successfully uses an innovative model to conduct its business.

The University of Rochester Press is now an established publisher of critically acclaimed scholarly work for an academic readership, fully staffed by editorial, production, and marketing professionals. With offices located in the University's historic Ellwanger-Barry Nursery building, the Press is a member of the Association of American University Presses.

The idea of a scholarly press for the University arose (almost certainly not for the first time) in the 1988–89 academic year as part of the usual and ongoing evaluation of academic programs and the synergies between them. In line with its peer institutions, scholarship and research that push the boundaries of knowledge have always been a vital part of the University's mission. Although University of Rochester faculty members were prodigious producers of scholarly work with various university presses around the nation, it seemed as if the University of Rochester was missing one element that would contribute to scholarship nationally and internationally. Not only could it have productive faculty, it could have its own scholarly press in service to the academy.

Initial thoughts about establishing such a press emerged in 1988–89 in conversations between President Dennis O'Brien and Provost Brian J. Thompson. And, as they tried out the idea on faculty leaders, it was clear that others wholeheartedly shared their enthusiasm. Such a press would enhance the University's contributions to the world of scholarship and, strategically, would add particular value if the Press were to publish in fields where the University was already strong. During such discussions O'Brien and Thompson were actually reminded by colleagues with long memories that there had *been* a University of Rochester

Press at one time. That operation had been based in Rush Rhees Library and had produced the Microcard Series, containing material previously published in print form as well as a series of theses that had not been formally published. An article in the *University Record* in 1961, titled "Micropublication Grows," told how this earlier press was formed:

> In 1953 an anonymous grant of $45,000 was given to the University for publishing. The subscriber response has been so encouraging that, although it was believed that the grant would last three years, enough funds have been earned to turn back into service to enable publication to continue.

This in fact speaks to one of the traditional ways of starting a scholarly press—that is, by having a significant endowment to support the activity. In this case, however, the funds were not sufficient for a traditional endowment, but served as operational funding for a limited period.

A second statement in the same article is also worthy of note: "Rush Rhees Library is spreading the name of the University not only throughout the country but into many areas of the world. . . . Subscribers include . . . University of Tasmania and Technische Hogeschool in Deft. Recently added is Tanganyika." This was a significant benefit of the enterprise. By serving as a center for disseminating the work of scholars, the University was able to add to the ways in which its name was spread among academic institutions internationally.

The newly formed press remained a successful venture for some sixteen years (1953–68), but it was not a scholarly press of the profile that would be most useful to the

University in the late 1980s. In the discussions of 1988
and 1989, all involved could see the advantages of having a
true scholarly press with foci fine enough to help build the
University's reputation. It was also important that the Press
be related to the whole University and have a direct cou-
pling to all of the colleges and schools—hence the concept
that, if formed, the enterprise would be the responsibility
of the provost's office. The Press would publish in academic

Margaret Toth, editor of the University of Rochester Press Micropublication
Service (1953–68), assisting a library patron. Courtesy of the Department of
Rare Books and Special Collections, Rush Rhees Library, University of
Rochester Library.

MICROCARD PUBLICATIONS
THE FIRST "UNIVERSITY OF ROCHESTER PRESS"

This press was in operation from 1953 to 1968. It published material on microcards; a three-hundred-page book would take up no more than three microcards, each 3 x 5 inches in size. Subject matter included library sciences (the Association of College and Research Libraries Series included 125 titles, mostly master's theses from many places in the country and a few monographs). The music series was successful: "in one music series are mostly [Eastman School of Music] doctoral dissertations, [and] rare music literature was also reproduced, including Praetorius Syntagma Musicum."

disciplines relating to the strengths of the University with volumes authored by scholars from academic institutions around the world, and ideally would publish the work of some of the University's own scholars as well.

An alternative to raising a sizeable endowment for the Press—a course of action not available at the time—would be to use the University's regular internal accounts to provide the start-up funding and to bear the annual costs for staff salaries and benefits, equipment, and operations. These annual costs would start to be covered once books had been published and sold. In short, the Press could be a significant line item in the University's budget. At the time, however, many universities (including Rochester) were facing considerable budgetary constraints. Also, a number of university presses that had been founded on this model were not able to generate sufficient annual revenues to cover annual costs, let alone return the original investment.

With neither an endowment nor a sizeable operating budget from institutional coffers a ready possibility, the University began to explore other models, such as contractual arrangements with other scholarly publishers and, particularly, with other university presses. This, however, would require significant financial investment from the University's partner; even with reduced annual costs, one or another of the parties involved would inevitably be exposed to financial risk.

But O'Brien, Thompson, and others were determined not to give up on a good idea. Would some small, high-quality scholarly press be willing to become a strategic business partner? After a few inconclusive conversations with other entities, a group of faculty including professors Thomas Hahn and Russell Peck of the English department—significantly involved with medieval history and literature—suggested approaching Boydell & Brewer, Ltd., a British company privately owned and with a strong reputation for publishing serious scholarly work. Thus an introduction was made and a meeting scheduled in Rochester to discuss the possibilities. Dr. Richard Barber, one of the founders of the company and its managing director, and Professor Derek Brewer, medieval literature scholar and the other founder of Boydell & Brewer, were willing participants in the discussions. Brewer at that time was Master of Emmanuel College at Cambridge University, well published, and the foremost expert of his day on Chaucer. Barber was (and still is) a prolific scholar with books on King Arthur, knights and chivalry, tournaments, and other medieval topics. (His definitive book on the

Holy Grail was released in the U.S., to acclaim, in 2004 by Harvard University Press.)

Barber and Brewer had already incorporated Boydell & Brewer, Inc., in the United States in May of 1986 as the firm prepared to develop more direct opportunities for its sales and marketing efforts and interaction with the scholarly community on this side of the Atlantic. After further discussion, both sides enthusiastically agreed that they had found the perfect strategic partner for their respective objectives.

All that remained was to negotiate and draw up the details of the agreement, and with the involvement of B&B solicitors and the University lawyers prepare documents for signatures. The agreement was signed by all parties on June 21, 1989, with an effective date of September 1, 1989. ✍

chapter 2

The Agreement

A<small>N AGREEMENT WAS SIGNED ON</small> J<small>UNE</small> 21, 1989, by the University of Rochester, Boydell & Brewer Limited (B&B Ltd.) registered in England, and Boydell & Brewer, Inc. (B&B Inc.), incorporated in New Hampshire. Three formal "whereas" statements set out the objective.

WHEREAS

(A) In pursuit of the University's professed aim to promote learning, to disseminate knowledge, to publish scholarly works by and for the University's faculty, students, and other constituents, and in particular to publish works which would not be considered by more commercially minded publishers, the University desires to establish a press to be operated by the University for the purpose of publishing educational works in the humanities and sciences under the imprint "University of Rochester Press" ("URP"); and

(B) B & B Ltd. is a publisher of specialist academic and historical works in the United Kingdom and B & B Inc. is a wholly-owned subsidiary of B & B Ltd.

> Established for the purpose of promoting the sale
> of B & B Ltd. publications in the USA; and
>
> (C) B & B Ltd. and B & B Inc. (hereinafter together
> referred to as "B & B") have agreed with the Univer-
> sity to provide URP with publishing services on the
> terms hereinafter set forth. . . .

The remainder of the agreement formally set out the responsibilities of the partners to the University of Rochester Press.

The partnership needed careful definition. The editorial board of URP would take full responsibility for determining the scope of the publishing profile in various disciplines, approving series editors and any series advisory boards. The URP editorial director would bring to the editorial board, for discussion and decision, proposals that the editor had accepted for consideration and that had undergone peer review. This is, of course, standard practice for any university press, but was spelled out in detail to underscore the way in which editorial decisions remained under University direction despite the arrangement with an outside publishing house for production, marketing, and distribution. The editorial board, made up largely of University faculty, was to be appointed by the provost and chaired by the provost or the provost's designee. The University did, however, also wish to get professional input from the experienced scholars and publishers at B&B. Hence, Richard Barber and Derek Brewer were appointed to the board by the provost. This action was written into the agreement so that B&B could continue to nominate "two qualified persons to serve on the editorial board." The editorial board is also responsible for the selection of the editorial director.

Once a manuscript had been approved, manuscript editing would be the responsibility of the Press editor, and then the Boydell & Brewer staff members would oversee production management, printing, warehousing, invoicing and accounting services, marketing, promotion and sales, and distribution to a worldwide market. B&B would bear all the costs incurred in fulfilling these obligations, and would retain the revenue from sales, returning to the University a negotiated percentage of its income from worldwide sales of URP books.

The University would provide and pay for suitable offices and facilities on University grounds, and also support a limited amount of secretarial support service and a phone line.

As noted, the agreement called for the editorial board to recommend the appointment of the Press's editor. Until such time as the editor might be appointed and employed full time by the University, the appointee would be employed by Boydell & Brewer and compensated by that firm. However, the editor also would have a nonstipendiary appointment from the University to recognize that he or she was serving at the pleasure of the editorial board and under its general guidance and direction. (Years later, the editor's position would indeed become a staff position within the provost's office under terms stated in the original agreement.)

Following the signing of the agreement, a set of "schedules to the agreement" was prepared covering four areas: editorial; production; invoicing, accounting, and warehousing; and promotion and marketing. These schedules further defined the interface between the University of Rochester Press and Boydell & Brewer.

A great deal of care and attention was paid to drafting the original agreement and schedules, which have withstood the test of time: twenty years later the parties still operate under their terms.

At the outset, the arrangement was not entirely without risk. Even as an independent and well-respected scholarly publisher, Boydell & Brewer was nonetheless a commercial operation. It was critical that the nascent University of Rochester Press maintain its integrity as a true university press and ensure that commercial considerations not consciously or unconsciously overwhelm its mission. By placing editorial control squarely with the University, both partners made sure that would happen.

At the same time, the new collaboration was greatly strengthened by the fact that Boydell & Brewer was not a typical commercial operation; the company still remained in private hands and was committed to intellectual as much as commercial profit. Further, the presence of two B&B representatives on the editorial board—originally Barber and Brewer, both scholars in their own right—ensured that there would be an ongoing process to allow the firm to participate appropriately in the editorial process.

The University of Rochester Press became a reality on September 1, 1989, and was publicly announced by press release on September 11, together with a front page article in the University publication *Currents* with the headline "University and British firm team up to run a new press." President O'Brien said, "Reaching out to the global community of scholars with our own press is a tremendously important undertaking. This addition helps us extend our research mission by making available new knowledge to the

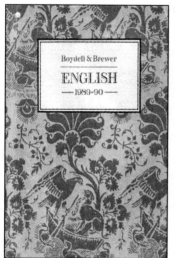

Covers of two Boydell & Brewer catalogs at the time of our agreement.

rest of the world. Before undertaking this enterprise, however, we looked for a partner who could guide us in the production and marketing end of publishing. I believe we've found the best possible colleague in Boydell & Brewer."

One not unimportant consequence of the arrangement with B&B is that the University brought a new international company to Rochester, New York. Today, B&B, Inc., employs twelve staff members in its Rochester office.

All in all, it was an unusual way for a university to start a scholarly press—without first raising a sustaining endowment or preparing to incur substantial operational costs. It relied on the good fortune of finding just the right partner, in this case an internationally established scholarly publisher looking for a foothold in the United States. Over the years, the arrangement has proven its considerable benefits both

BOYDELL & BREWER IN 1989: A BRIEF PROFILE

When the University of Rochester Press was established, Boydell & Brewer Ltd. had been in existence for twenty years. It had developed from very modest beginnings into a scholarly publisher of note, under the direction of Derek Brewer, professor of English and Master of Emmanuel College, Cambridge, and independent scholar Richard Barber, whose principal interest was history. Its specialty was medieval studies, and it often published works rejected as not viable on commercial terms by the university presses of the period. Boydell also published general trade titles, and the company had just begun its involvement with the highly acclaimed Spanish literature list, Tamesis Books, founded by Professor John Varey of the University of London, which was doing similar work in the academic field. It had also begun to distribute for a number of English learned societies, including the major series of monographs begun by Professor Sir Geoffrey Elton for the Royal Historical Society.

Boydell & Brewer Ltd. was based in Woodbridge, Suffolk, and was privately owned, with backing from Investors in Industry (3i), one of the earliest and biggest venture capital companies. It operated in the U.S. through the newly-created office in Rochester and used a distribution service in Fitchburg, Massachusetts, to reach the U.S. market. Unusually, the company always retained world rights to its titles, rather than subcontracting to a U.S. company, on the grounds that there was not sufficient margin in specialist academic titles for two publishers to be involved. The policy continues to this day and is applied equally to University of Rochester Press titles.

both to the University and to Boydell & Brewer. Moreover, in an era when many university presses have fallen on hard times (or worse) this unusual model for operations shows a nontraditional approach to an enduring responsibility of educational institutions: to give scholars the broadest possible voice.

chapter 3

The Press Is Launched

WORK BEGAN QUICKLY to get the basic structure for the new university press in place. Space was allocated in the University of Rochester's administration building (now Wallis Hall) on the River Campus; the Press found its first home in a basement office that could be expanded to two offices when needed. The provost agreed to take the leadership role for the University by chairing the editorial board and appointing board members in order to start formulating the directions of the Press. Founding board members were Donald Kelley, Marie Curran Wilson and Joseph Chamberlain Wilson Professor of European History; Asish Basu, professor of geology and chair of the department; John P. McGowan, associate professor of English at the Eastman School of Music; and Boydell & Brewer's Richard Barber and Derek Brewer.

Once the agreement with the University was signed, Robert Easton was recruited in the United Kingdom to join the staff of Boydell & Brewer as URP's first editor. Starting in 1989, he spent his first three months in the B&B office in England and then transferred to the Rochester office. (Easton stayed until 1995; he was succeeded by Sean

Culhane, 1995–98, Timothy Madigan, 1999–2004, and Suzanne E. Guiod, 2004 to the present.)

Instrumental in Easton's appointment, Barber also fulfilled his responsibility to set up Boydell & Brewer offices on campus in his role as managing director of the UK company of which B&B, Inc., was a subsidiary. A valuable aspect of the new agreement was that the Press effectively and instantly had an office in England—the sales and marketing office that served the rest of the world even as North American sales were handled from the Rochester office, thereby giving all University of Rochester Press books international distribution. Of course, B&B, Inc., had to put in place its own organization for production management from acceptance of the manuscripts to delivery of bound books, warehousing, invoicing and accounting services, marketing and sales, and related services.

The members of the editorial board and Robert Easton had many informal discussions in planning for the future and preparing the agenda for the first formal meeting on November 8, 1989.

The direction of the Press was stated formally in a news release and general solicitation for proposals:

Following its inaugural meeting on November 8th, the editorial board of the University of Rochester Press is now actively seeking proposals for its first publications, and for longer-term projects. The basic principles under which we will operate are as follows:

1. Our publishing program will be based on subject areas in which the University is recognized as a major academic force or on academic works and

　　　　projects which derive from the special scholarly
　　　　strengths of the region.
2.　　We are looking to develop a list that features books
　　　　in specific subject areas, particularly those which are
　　　　not widely published elsewhere.
3.　　We are specially interested in proposals from poten-
　　　　tial editors of series which come under the guide-
　　　　lines stated above.

From the start, a university press must pay attention to building a reputation for publishing intellectually rigorous, full-vetted works of scholarship. Even as details of the Press were being ironed out and the staff put in place, the board had begun to give significant thought to launching the publications in a set of offerings, preferably in series, in disciplines of the University's academic strengths. Professor Donald Kelley and editor Robert Easton developed the first series that the board was pleased to accept and endorse when it reviewed the details at its first formal meeting on November 8, 1989.

The Library of the History of Ideas

Donald Kelley was at the time the executive editor of the *Journal of the History of Ideas.* The plan was to organize a series of thematic volumes of selected articles from the journal with each volume edited by a noted scholar. A series editor appointed by the board would have overall responsibility for the series. Thus the Library of the History of Ideas became a series of volumes on major themes of intellectual history, drawn from selected articles published in the *Journal of the History of Ideas* since its founding in 1940.

John W. Yolton, John Locke Professor History and Philosophy at Rutgers University, accepted the appointment as series editor and twelve volumes were planned. Appropriately, Kelley agreed to edit volume one, titled *The History of Ideas: Canons and Variations.* The series was announced in 1990 and volumes one and two appeared in that year.

Two volumes were published in 1991: *Hume as Philosopher of Society, Politics and History,* edited by Donald Livingston and Marie Martin, and *Race, Class and Gender in Nineteenth-Century Culture* with Maryanne Cline Horowitz as the editor. Four volumes were published in 1992 and three in 1993, including *Renaissance Essays,* which had been in the editors' sights from the inception. The story is best told in the preface by editor Paul Oskar Kirsteller:

> The volume entitled *Renaissance Essays from the Journal of the History of Ideas,* edited by the late Professor Philip P. Wiener and myself and published by Harper & Row as a Harper Torchbook in 1968, has recently gone out of print, and the copyright has reverted to the *Journal of the History of Ideas.* I was pleased to learn that the University of Rochester Press, in agreement with the editors of the *Journal,* is willing to reprint the original volume, including its introduction, as volume IX of the series, Library of the History of Ideas. It contains a number of articles which have achieved classic, and in some cases (notably that of Meyer Schapiro), controversial status. A new volume, to be edited by Professor William J. Connell in consultation with Professor Donald R. Kelley, will be published later in the same series. It will include a number of more recent renaissance articles from the *Journal,* and thus bring also the earlier articles up to date. I should like to thank the

University of Rochester Press and its director, Mr. Robert M. Easton, and the editors of the *Journal,* and especially Professors Donald R. Kelley, John W. Yolton and William J. Connell, for their willingness to make this volume again available. I hope the new edition will be received as favorably as the earlier one. . . .

The last title appeared in 1994 to complete the twelve volumes that had been planned. The Press then made it a baker's dozen with a thirteenth volume in 1995, *Language and the History of Thought* by Nancy Struever.

Acquiring the UMI List

Late in 1989 UMI Research Press, an imprint of University Microfilms, Inc., in Michigan, decided that certain book publishing activities no longer fit within its overall strategic plan. After some extended discussions in 1990 with UMI, the University of Rochester Press signed a "sales agreement" for stock of fifty-two titles from several lists of interest to URP that would align with its own strategic directions. These lists were Studies in Music, Russian Music Studies, Nineteenth-Century Studies, and Challenging the Literary Canon.

The stock of these titles was transferred to the warehouse in January and February of 1991, and individual volumes were available to be shipped in March. A number of volumes were also reprinted, including such titles as:

> *The Letters and Documents of Heinrich Schultz, 1656–1672: An Annotated Translation* by Gina Spognoli (1992)

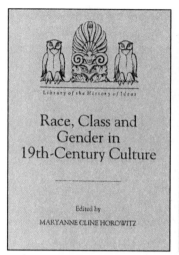

Two covers of volumes in the Library of the History of Ideas

New Essays on Performance Practice by Frederick Neumann. (1992)

German Music Theory in the Early 17th Century by B. Rivera (1994)

Opera and Drama in Russia in the 1860s by R. Taruskin (1994)

American Women Composers before 1870 by J. Tick (1995)

A Reception–History of George Eliot's Fiction J. Russell Perkin (1995)

Other titles, including *Hugo Wolf's Lieder and Extensions of Tonality* (O.J. Stein) and *Russian Theoretical Thought in Music* (edited by G. D. McQuere), remain available through print-on-demand technology.

LIBRARY OF THE HISTORY OF IDEAS

The History of Ideas: Canon and Variations, edited by Donald R. Kelley (1990)

Philosophy, Religion and Science in the Seventeenth and Eighteenth Century, edited by John W. Yolton (1990)

Race, Class and Gender in Nineteenth-Century Culture, edited by Maryanne Cline Horowitz (1991)

Hume as Philosopher of Society, Politics and History, edited by Donald Livingston and Marie Martin (1991)

Essays on History of Aesthetics, edited by Peter Kivy (1992)

Essays on Political Philosophy, edited by Patrick Riley (1992)

Discovering China: European Interpretations in the Enlightenment, edited by Julia Ching and Willard G. Oxtoby (1992)

Race, Gender, and Rank: Early Modern Ideas of Humanity, edited by Maryanne Cline Horowitz (1992)

Renaissance Essays, edited by Paul Oskar Kristeller and Philip P. Wiener (first published by Harper & Row, 1968)

Renaissance Essays II, edited by William J. Connell (1993)

The American Enlightenment, edited by Frank Shuffelton (1993)

Figures on the Horizon, edited by Jerrold Seigel (1994)

Language and the History of Thought, edited by Nancy Struever (1995)

In addition to the original fifty-two titles, the Press was able to reissue a number of titles from the various UMI series. These acquisitions decidedly moved URP and B&B forward in the marketplace; the Press name was recognized as a more significant participant in the world of scholarly publishing. At the same time, the Press provided a service to those scholars whose work continued to be available and be promoted.

The Link Foundation Program

The Link Foundation was established in 1953 by Edwin A. and Marion C. Link as a New York Charitable Trust. Link was best known for his invention of the first successful flight simulator in 1929. The mission of the Link Foundation is "to perpetuate and enhance the recognized Link legacy of technical leadership and excellence established by the founders in their fields of interest—simulation and training, energy resources development and conservation, and ocean engineering and instrumentation—while also continuing the support of organizations consistent with the founders' interests."

As a result of strong ties between the University and the Link Foundation over a number of years, the University was asked in 1983 to advise the foundation on a program for a national competition for PhD student fellowships in the energy field. The University would ultimately manage and implement the new program, with the first group of Link Foundation Energy Fellowships awarded for the 1984–85 academic year. Initially, annual conferences were held in Rochester at which fellows reported on their research and also submitted a written paper. The papers were informally

Covers of published volumes from the UMI list.

published by the University of Rochester on behalf of the Link Foundation under the title Proceedings of the Annual Link Conference on Energy. The first book contained the papers from the 1985 and 1986 conferences, labeled as volumes one and two. Volume three was printed in 1987. Volumes four and five were were issued by the University under the title *Reports of the Link Energy Fellows* in 1988 and 1989 respectively. A limited number of these volumes were produced and donated to a list of research libraries.

The acceptance and success of these volumes suggested to the foundation that the University should be more formal in the processing and publication of the reports. Consequently, the guidelines for the submission of reports were revised so that papers would have a consistent format and would be similar to articles submitted to a scholarly journal. Provost Thompson was responsible for the overall program and agreed to be the editor for future volumes. Volume six was carried out under these guidelines even though most of the papers had been submitted under the old rules. This volume was edited and published by the University of Rochester Press in association with the Link Foundation in 1990.

Subsequent volumes changed in format and all submissions were standardized under the new guidelines and style; they were edited and accepted for publication often after significant revisions. Volume seven was the first of these 6 x 9 inch books. Enough copies were printed to be donated by the foundation to most of the major research libraries in North America. The series continued until volume fifteen in 1999.

Based on the success of the Energy Fellowship Program, the Link Foundation launched two similar programs. The first was Simulation and Training managed by the Institute for Simulation and Training at the University of Central Florida; the second a few years later in Ocean Engineering and Instrumentation was managed for the foundation by Florida Institute of Technology's Division of Marine and Environmental Systems. The responsibility for the Energy Fellowship Program is currently at the Thayer School of Engineering at Dartmouth College. (Professor Lee Lynd, current leader of the program, was a Link Energy Fellow in the very first year, twenty-five years earlier!)

A new series of volumes was started in 2001 with three parts, one for each of the foundation's disciplinary areas, edited and published by the Press for the foundation. URP involvement with the publication part of the program ended in 2005. It had been an extensive and valuable partnership providing support for the Press in its formative years, and enhancing the Link Fellowship program.

ENERGY

SIMULATION-TRAINING

OCEAN ENGINEERING AND INSTRUMENTATION

Research Papers of the Link Foundation Fellows
Volume 3

Brian J. Thompson, Editor

50th Anniversary
1953-2003

Published by
The University of Rochester Press
in Association with
The Link Foundation

Volume 3 of the *Research Papers of the Link Foundation Fellows*, 2003, for the 50th anniversary of the founding of the Link Foundation.

Some Special Initiatives

Rochester Symposium on Developmental Psychopathology

Professor Dante Cicchetti of the University of Rochester pioneered the discipline of developmental psychopathology, which led to the founding of the annual Rochester Symposium on Developmental Psychopathology in 1987 and also the establishment of the University's Mt. Hope Family Center. The first symposium had the title "The Emergence of a Discipline." The second annual symposium, "Internalizing and Externalizing Expressions of Dysfunction," was held in 1988. Both symposia proceedings were published by Lawrence Erlbaum Associates Inc. in 1989 and 1991 respectively. Cicchetti edited the first volume and he and Sheree L. Toth, an associate at the Mt. Hope Family Center, edited the second.

The Press then published a number of volumes between 1991 and 1999 resulting from each annual Rochester Symposium on Developmental Psychopathology and edited by Cicchetti and Toth, with the following titles:

Models and Integrations

Developmental Perspectives on Depression

Disorders and Dysfunctions of the Self

Emotion, Cognition and Representation

Adolescence: Opportunities and Challenges

Developmental Perspectives on Trauma

Theory, Research and Interventions

Developmental Approach to Prevention and Intervention

These works comprise a very significant library of what at the time were the latest results and thinking on developmental psychopathology—one example of the Press publishing in subject areas in which the University is recognized for its strengths.

Trophoblast Research

Between 1992 and 1999, the Press had the privilege of publishing a series of international conference proceedings on trophoblast research (relating to the outermost layer of a fertilized egg as it adheres to the uterine wall) under the general editorship of Professors Richard K. Miller and Henry A. Thiede of the University's School of Medicine and Dentistry. Visible success with this series led to other stand-alone volumes in the field of science and medicine, often as a result of other international conferences.

Other Specialized Volumes

Other specialized works included the following:

Basic and Applied High Pressure Biology edited by P. B. Bennett and R. E. Marquis (1994), an outcome of a meeting organized by the International Group on High Pressure Biology held at Duke University in June 1992.

High Pressure Biology and Medicine edited by P. B. Bennett, Ivan Demchenko and R. E. Marquis (1998) on the Fifth International Meeting on High Pressure Biology, St. Petersburg, Russia.

Strongly Coupled Plasma Physics edited by H. M. Van Horn and S. Ichimara (1993) on an international conference held in Rochester in 1992.

Cariology for the Nineties edited by William H. Bowen and Lawrence A. Tabak (1993), the proceedings of a conference by the same name held at the University of Rochester in 1991.

The Editorial Board meeting in the fall of 1990. Back row: Barber, Basu, Kelley and Easton; front row: Thompson, McGowan, Brewer. The photograph on the wall is of Robert L. Sproull, president emeritus of the University, whose book *Scientist's Tools for Business* was published by the Press in 1997.

Robert Sproull, former President of the University of Rochester, whose book *Scientist's Tools for Business* was cited as a finalist in the how-to book category for the 1997 Financial Times/Booz-Allen & Hamilton Global Business Book Awards.

chapter 4

THE LIST THROUGH THE YEARS

ESPECIALLY BEFORE THE FIRM ESTABLISHMENT of the range of series that now largely define the University of Rochester Press's publishing program, the general list served as an important developmental aspect of the Press's portfolio. It consisted of a number of parts: projects that pointed towards future series or that were published in tandem with a series; volumes that supported a number of the University's special academic interests and activities; and high profile books that had a significant Rochester profile or author. Some notable examples are mentioned here.

> *Court, Country and Culture: Essays on Early Modern British History in honor of Perez Zagorin,* edited by Bonnelyn Young Kunze and Dwight D. Brautigam (1992). Focusing on the political, intellectual, and cultural context of England in the early modern period (fourteenth century to eighteenth century), this volume of essays honoring Peter Zagorin, Wilson Professor Emeritus of History, University of Rochester, in part represents the breadth of his wide-ranging work and intellectual interests. These studies explore political theory and

the English revolution, the revisionist debates over the court and the country, and the role of Laudian policies in the years prior to the Civil War. (Boydell & Brewer published Zagorin's book *Milton, Aristocrat & Rebel: The Poet and His Policies* under the D. S. Brewer imprint also in 1992.

Cold Fusion: The Scientific Fiasco of the Centuries, by John R. Huizenga (1993). In the spring of 1989, two electrochemists claimed to have duplicated the high-temperature process powering the sun, at room temperature, in a small jar on a laboratory tabletop, although subsequently their results could not be replicated. In addition to analyzing cold fusion reports, Huizenga explored the hazards of going public with a far-reaching promise without sufficient experimental evidence. "Huizenga has written an authoritative, frank, hard-hitting account of the cold fusion fiasco. He compares this with other examples of pathological science and makes suggestions for the proper operation of the scientific process."—Glenn T. Seaborg, Nobel Laureate in Chemistry, University of California at Berkeley. (This timely book turned out to be a best seller, leading to features in the magazine *Nature* and on the television program NOVA.)

Working Toward Freedom: Slave Society and Domestic Economy in the American South, edited by Larry E. Hudson (1995). Drawing from a range of primary sources, these essays show how slaves organized their domestic economy and created an economic and social space for themselves under slavery which profoundly affected family and gender relations. This was an important

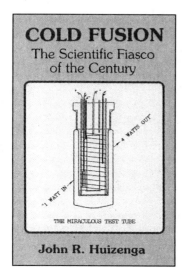

volume for the URP, which had decided to focus on this subject area. The work presaged the launch of the very successful series Rochester Studies in African History and the Diaspora. A paperback edition of *Working Toward Freedom* was published in 1995.

Head, Heart and Hand: Elbert Hubbard and The Roycrofters by Marie Via and Marjorie B. Searl (1994). This illustrated catalogue accompanied the University of Rochester Memorial Art Gallery's exhibition of the same name, the first major assemblage of objects produced at the Roycroft community in upstate New York under the leadership of the charismatic Elbert Hubbard. The exhibition opened in Rochester on October 30, 1994, and traveled to the Akron (Ohio) Art Museum, Allentown (Pennsylvania) Art Museum, Frederick R.

Weisman Museum of Art at Pepperdine University in Malibu, California, Virginia Museum of Fine Art in Richmond, Virginia, and New York State Museum in Albany, New York. This association with the Memorial Art Gallery led to a number of other collaborative projects as well as some independent publications on art and artists, and on photography.

Carl W. Peters: American Scene Painter from Rochester to Rockport, by Richard H. Love (1999). This book provided a detailed analysis of the history of American Scene painting and Regionalism with an emphasis on artists active during the period between the two world wars. In conjunction with this publication, some twenty-seven paintings were loaned by the author for public exhibition in Rochester at the Century Club, a private women's club on East Avenue. Further, this volume became the three-millionth-and-first book acquired by the University of Rochester Libraries—formally received on April 13, 1999 (along with the three-millionth volume, *Lies! Lies! Lies!,* a college journal of the late novelist John Gardner, newly published by the libraries in association with Boa Editions, Ltd.).

The Press has continued to support the Memorial Art Gallery by distributing and marketing some of the fine art publications the Gallery has prepared, designed, and published. One such volume, *Voices in the Gallery: Writers on Art,* was published as a Press title and marketed outside the local area to garner wider publicity for and recognition of the Gallery. An exceptionally fine volume produced by the

the university of rochester press
presentation to the libraries

the **three-million-first** *volume to be added to the collections*
is being presented to the libraries by the university of rochester press,
which has just celebrate the publication of its first **100 titles**.
the press is providing the first copy of
the newly published book,

carl w. peters: american scene painter from rochester to rockport,
as part of the three millionth volume celebration.
written by richard h. love,
the book chronicles the work and career of the rochester-born peters,
recognized as a **pioneer amerian scene painter** *and regionist.*

In 1999, *Carl W. Peters: American Scene Painter from Rochester to Rockport*
was presented to the University Libraries as part of the ceremony for the
acquisition of the libraries' "three millionth commemorative volumes." It
was listed as the "three-millionth-first volume."

Gallery in 2006 was *Seeing America: Painting and Sculpture from the Collection of the Memorial Art Gallery of the University of Rochester.* This book was dedicated to the memory of Gertrude Herdle Moore, legendary Gallery director, and Isabel Herdle, associate director and curator, and additionally honored current gallery director Grant Holcomb on the twentieth anniversary of his directorship. The Press again was the distributor of this work.

The Illuminating Mind in American Photography: Stieglitz, Strand, Weston, Adams, by David P. Peeler (2001). This work examines the ideas, images, and lives of these four major twentieth century American photographers. "Focusing on Stieglitz, Strand, Weston, and Ansel Adams, Peeler's [work] examines this central group of modernist photographers with extraordinary insight and depth. His lucid narrative weaves together biography and cultural history, revealing the fascinating interconnections between these photographers, while maintaining its chief interest in the evolution of their individual photographic modes."—Miles Orvell, professor of English and American studies, Temple University.

Picturing Performance: The Iconography of the Performing Arts in Concept and Practice, by Thomas F. Heck (1999). Aspiring iconographers of the performing arts need to be aware that there are often several levels of interpretation which great works of visual art will sustain. This book explores these levels of interpretation: a surface or literal reading, a deeper reading of the work which seeks to enter the mind of the artist and asks how and why he put a given work together, and the deepest reading of

HEAD, HEART AND HAND
ELBERT HUBBARD AND
THE ROYCROFTERS

MARIE VIA AND MARJORIE SEARL

The **Illuminating**
Mind
in
American
Photography

Stieglitz, Strand, Weston, Adams

By David P. Peeler

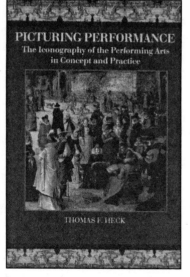

PICTURING PERFORMANCE
The Iconography of the Performing Arts
in Concept and Practice

THOMAS F. HECK

the work relating it to the artistic traditions and culture in which the artist lived. "Picturing Performance ranks as one of the outstanding arts resources for the new millennium. Heck and the contributors effectively define and theorize on the iconography of performance, while also providing voluminous practical information on locating and 'reading' visual imagery in music, theatre, dance, and other performing arts."—James Fisher, professor of theater, Wabash College.

Literary Adaptations in Black American Cinema, from Micheaux to Morrison, by Barbara Tepa Lupack (2002). The author's work reveals that while blacks, on screen and behind the scenes, were often forced to recreate demeaning film stereotypes, they learned how to subvert and exploit the artificiality of their caricatures. "Beautifully crafted, meticulously researched, comprehensive in scope, exhaustive in detail, this fine critical history of film adaptations of black literature represents a significant contribution to this field and an essential resource for future scholars."—Barry H. Leeds, Distinguished Connecticut State University Professor of English, Connecticut State University.

Hollywood's Film Wars with France: Film-Trade Diplomacy and the Emergence of the French Film Quota Policy, by Jens Ulff–Møller (2001). The book examines how Hollywood was able to establish a permanent dominance over the French market for motion pictures. "As Ulff–Møller shows, politics, diplomacy, and aggressive trade practices played an extraordinary role as early as the First World War in giving American film studios

Literary Adaptations in Black American Cinema:

from Micheaux to Morrison

Barbara Tepa Lupack

HOLLYWOOD'S FILM WARS WITH FRANCE

FILM TRADE DIPLOMACY AND THE EMERGENCE OF THE FRENCH FILM QUOTA POLICY

Jens Ulff-Møller

Women Television Producers 1948-2000

Robert Alley and Irby Brown

huge advantages in Europe. Students of film, business, and French-American relations will find much to ponder in this absorbing story of cultural combat and market manipulation."—Herrick Chapman, professor of French studies, New York University.

Women Television Producers 1948–2000, by Robert Alley and Irby Brown (2002). The focus of this work is on a new cadre of woman producers, who, as a result of rulings by the Equal Employment Opportunities Commission in the early seventies, found employment in the three major networks beginning in 1971–72. In the following decade many of them emerged as television producers and writers. "This first serious look at women television producers could only have been put together by Bob Alley and Irby Brown, who have spent 25 years investigating and assessing the 'scene' in Los Angeles. They have had access to virtually every important director, producer, network and studio executive—making this book indispensable for the study of television history and the role women played in shaping it."—Suzanne W. Jones, editor of *Writing the Woman Artist* and *Crossing the Color Line: Reading in Black and White.*

Medical Books

Given the outstanding strength of the University of Rochester medical school and its affiliate Strong Memorial Hospital, it is not surprising that the Press saw a responsibility to publish in this broad field of basic science and clinical practice. Early work in this area was described in the previous chapter.

Publishing in medicine continued with two volumes in 1997: *Polio,* edited by Thomas M. Daniel and Frederick C. Robbins, and *Captain of Death: The Story of Tuberculosis* by Thomas M. Daniel. Paperback editions followed in subsequent years and demand continues for these titles. Others have included:

Post-War Mothers: Childbirth Letters to Grantly Dick-Read, 1946–1956, by Mary Alvey Thomas (1998). This edited collection of correspondence affords a rare look at childbirth experiences in the hospitals and birthing centers in post-war America and Britain from the perspective of the patient.

The Royal Doctors 1485–1714: Medical Personnel at the Tudor and Stuart Courts, by Elizabeth Lane Furdell (2001). More than three hundred men (and a handful of women), previously unexamined as a group, made up the medical staff of the Tudor and Stuart kings and queens of England (as well as the Lord Protectorships of Oliver and Richard Cromwell). The royal doctors faced enormous challenges in the sixteenth and seventeenth centuries from diseases that respected no rank and threatened the very security of the realm.

Presidential Disability: Papers and Discussions on Inability and Disability Among U.S. Presidents, edited by James F. Toole and Robert J. Joynt (2001). This book consists of the proceedings of a series of conferences held by the Working Group on Disability in US Presidents. Working group members—medical doctors, politicians, and former administration members—examined the

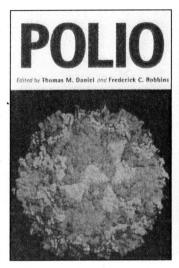

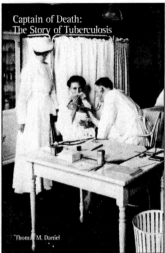

implications of the 25th Amendment to the United States Constitution. The working group, which received national attention, had been convened in response to an invitation by President Jimmy Carter to the American Academy of Neurology in 1994 and offered to the US Congress nine recommendations for the effective use of the Twenty-Fifth Amendment.

Wade Hampton Frost, Pioneer Epidemiologist 1880–1938: Up to the Mountain, by Thomas M. Daniel (2004). "Dr. Daniel's well written biography of Wade Hampton Frost brings to life the little known, yet inspirational story of one of public health's largely unsung heroes. Through his patient and thorough approach to understanding the nature and transmission of infectious diseases, Dr. Frost established the discipline of epidemiology and developed

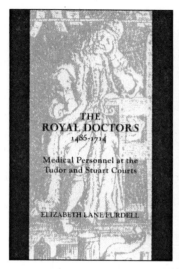

methods of analysis that form the basis of our efforts to prevent and control disease today."—C. William Keck, MD, MPH, past president of the American Public Health Association.

A vast collection housed in the University of Rochester Medical Center's Edward G. Miner Library formed the basis for a significant catalogue of materials on "popular medicine" in early America. Three volumes of *An Annotated Catalogue of the Edward C. Atwater Collection of American Popular Medicine and Health Reform* was compiled and annotated by Miner Library Rare Books and Manuscripts Librarian Christopher Hoolihan, in 2001, 2004, and 2008, and describe a variety of now-rare books written by physicians and other professionals to provide information for the nonmedical audience.

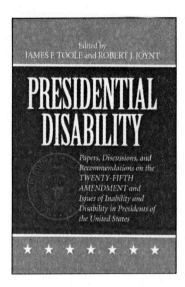

The introduction to volume three notes: "Dr. Atwater's initial gift of some twelve hundred titles in October 1994 has grown into a collection of more than seven thousand books, pamphlets, periodicals, almanacs, broadsides, circulars, trade cards, manuscripts, etc. in fourteen years. . . . Our purpose in publishing this catalog is to make the collection known to its actual beneficiaries, i.e., the scholars in many disciplines who will find in these volumes a detailed record of the efforts of ordinary Americans to control their own health."

This and other activities in the medical field led to the formation of the scholarly series Rochester Studies in Medical History (discussed in detail later), with Theodore M. Brown, professor of history at the University of Rochester and of community and preventative medicine at the University of Rochester Medical Center serving as series editor.

Eastman Studies in Music

Early on in the development of the Press, the world class reputation of the University of Rochester's Eastman School in Music made clear that a series of books on music history and theory would be an essential ingredient. Indeed, the Eastman Studies in Music series published its first books in 1994 with Ralph P. Locke, professor of musicology, as its energetic senior editor. A later section of this history is devoted to this series.

From time to time the Press has also published books on music outside the series when a project of interest didn't quite fit the profile for (or predated) the Eastman series. Such volumes included *A Yankee Musician in Europe: The 1837 Journals of Lowell Mason,* edited by Michael Broyles (1990); *The Wind Ensemble and its Repertoire: Essays on the Fortieth Anniversary of the Eastman Wind Ensemble,* edited by Frank J. Cipolla and Donald Hunsberger (1995); *Uncle Sam's Orchestra: Memories of the Seventh Army Symphony,* by John Canarina (1998); and *Wagner's* Meistersinger: *Performance, History Representation,* edited by Nicholas Vazsonyi (2003).

Other Special Publications

The Mismapping of America by Seymour I. Schwartz (2003) analyzes the significant cartographic errors that have shaped the history of the United States. Perhaps the most blatant error is the very name "America," which honors Amerigo Vespucci, who not only never set foot on North American soil, but also played no significant role in the discovery of South America. Other significant errors include Giovanni da Verrazzano's misinterpretation of Pamlico or Albermarle

Sound for the Pacific Ocean, thereby suggesting the presence of an isthmus in the middle of the North American continent; the existence of a direct North West passage between the Atlantic and Pacific oceans; the misconception that California was an island; and the insertion on Lake Superior of a fictitious island that is specifically referred to in defining the boundary of the United States. The thousandth copy was sold just five months after publication.

Window on Congress: A Congressional Biography of Barber B. Conable Jr., by James S. Fleming (2004) explores Conable's twenty-year congressional career, focusing on his remarkable educational abilities as a gifted teacher-legislator. It uses excerpts from Conable's private journal, newsletters and news columns, and information from personal interviews. Former Congressman and New York University President Emeritus John Brademas said that "Fleming has

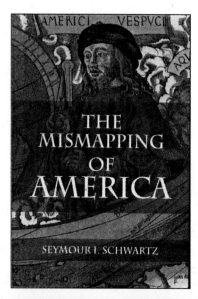

Dr. Seymour Schwartz celebrating the one-thousandth copy sold of *Mismapping of America*, with some of the staff of Boydell & Brewer and the University of Rochester Press. Left to right, Tim Madigan, Mark Klemens, Dr. Schwartz, Susan Dykstra-Poel, and Amy Powers.

illuminated our understanding of the crucial role of Congress in shaping national policy. With our separation-of-powers Constitution, when it comes to writing the nation's laws, Congress, unlike the legislature in a parliamentary system, counts! Fleming's splendid biography of Congressman Conable illustrates why."

From the Boardroom to the War Room: America's Corporate Liberals and FDR's Preparedness Program by Richard E. Holl (2005). Between World War I and World War II, America's corporate liberals experienced a profound ideological change. With the Great Depression, corporate liberals admitted that private efforts failed to maintain the nation's economic health, ultimately endorsing large-scale government intervention to bail out the stricken economy. By 1935, the corporate liberal conversion from privatism to business-government partnership was well under way.

Biographies

George Eastman: A Biography by Elizabeth Brayer (2006) represented a great (and appropriate) opportunity for the Press to publish the reprint edition of this important and definitive biography originally published by the Johns Hopkins University Press in 1996. Author Elizabeth Brayer is known for her writings about the history of central and western New York State. A second URP reprint of the Eastman biography was published in 2008. "Meticulously researched and clearly written, this book is unlikely to be rivaled and should be recognized as *the* standard work on the subject," wrote a *Bookshelf* reviewer. "Elizabeth Brayer should be congratulated on a magnificent achievement. A fitting tribute to one of the formative figures of modern times."

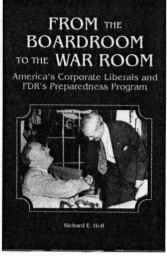

Going My Way: Bing Crosby and American Culture edited by Ruth Prigozy and Walter Raubicheck (2007) arose from a conference devoted to the life and career of Bing Crosby sponsored by the Hofstra Cultural Center and Hofstra University in 2002. In addition to studying Bing Crosby's innovations and remarkable achievements as a recording artist, *Going My Way* explores his accomplishments as an actor, businessman, and radio and television performer.

Frank Sinatra: The Man, the Music, the Legend edited by Jeanne Fuchs and Ruth Prigozy (2007) was the second volume derived from a successful conference held at Hofstra University and sponsored by the Hofstra Cultural Center. The contributors to this volume evaluate Sinatra's impact on all areas of entertainment, and examine many of the cultural forces he influenced and was influenced by, including Bing Crosby, Elvis, the "Beats," the Beatles, and Rock 'n' Roll.

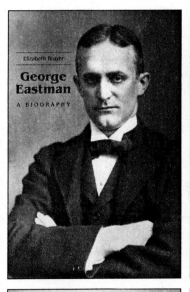

Elizabeth Brayer

George Eastman

A BIOGRAPHY

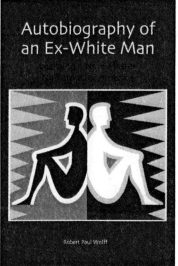

Autobiography of an Ex-White Man

Robert Paul Wolff

GOING **MY WAY**

BING CROSBY AND AMERICAN CULTURE

Edited by Ruth Prigozy & Walter Raubicheck

SINATRA

THE MAN, THE MUSIC, THE LEGEND

Edited by Jeanne Fuchs and Ruth Prigozy

Autobiography of an Ex-White Man: Learning a New Master Narrative for America by Robert Paul Wolff (2005) is an intensely personal meditation on the nature of America by a white philosopher who joined a black studies department at the University of Massachusetts and found his understanding of the world transformed by the experience.

A Profane Wit: The Life of John Wilmot, Earl of Rochester by James W. Johnson (2004) is an account of Rochester and his times, providing the facts behind the Earl of Rochester's legendary reputation as a rake and his deathbed repentance. However, it also demonstrates that he was a loving (if unfaithful) husband, a devoted father, a loyal friend, a serious scholar, a social critic, and an aspiring patriot.

The Serious Business
of Scholarly Series

A<small>T ITS VERY FIRST MEETING</small>, the editorial board clearly defined the goals for the Press. But as one might expect, it was a few years before the first series was actually launched—and more years before the series established themselves in depth and number.

Today, even as the Press continues to publish general titles, its list is largely defined by the growing reputations of its various specialized series throughout the greater academic community. And with two new series now anticipating inaugural volumes, the scope of the Press's publishing continues to expand.

Each series relies on a series editor (or co-editors) supported by an editorial advisory board. The series editor, in conjunction with the University of Rochester Press editorial director, defines the general thrust of the series and serves as chief solicitor and first reviewer of proposals. After review by the series editor and the series' editorial advisory board, further review by the Press editorial director, and a peer review process, each proposal goes before the Press editorial board for approval.

The first of these formal series initiated by the Press was launched in 1992–93, and others followed in due course.

Eastman Studies in Music

Series Editor: Ralph P. Locke, Professor of Musicology, Eastman School of Music
First title: *The Poetic Debussy* edited by Margaret G. Cobb (June 1994)

Rochester Studies in African History and the Diaspora

Series Editor: Toyin Falola, Frances Higginbotham Nalle Centennial Professor in History, University of Texas at Austin
First title: *Power Relations in Nigeria: Ilorin Slaves and Their Successors* by Ann O'Hear (October 1997)

Rochester Studies in Central Europe

Series Editor: Timothy Snyder, Professor of History, Yale University (Founding Editor: Ewa Hauser, Adjunct Associate Professor of Political Science, University of Rochester)
First title: *Post-Communist Transition: The Thorny Road* by Grzegorz W. Kolodko (October 2000)

Rochester Studies in Philosophy

Series Editor: Wade L. Robison, Ezra A. Hale Professor in Applied Ethics, Rochester Institute of Technology
First title: *The Scottish Enlightenment: Essays in Reinterpretation* edited by Paul Wood (November 2000)

Rochester Studies in Medical History

Series Editor: Theodore M. Brown, Professor of History and of Community and Preventive Medicine, University of Rochester
First title: *The Mechanization of the Heart: Harvey and Descartes* by Thomas Fuchs, translated from German by Marjorie Grene (October 2001)

Changing Perspectives on Early Modern Europe

Series Editor: James B. Collins, Professor of History, Georgetown University, and Mack P. Holt, Professor of History, George Mason University
First title: *Private Ambition and Political Alliances: The Phélypeaux de Pontchartrain Family and Louis XIV's Government 1650–1715* by Sara E. Chapman (May 2004)

Gender and Race in American History

Series Editor: Alison M. Parker, Associate Professor of History, State University College at Brockport, and Carol Faulkner, Associate Professor of History, Syracuse University
Established 2008, first title forthcoming

Eastman/Rochester Studies in Ethnomusicology

Series Editor: Ellen Koskoff, Professor of Ethnomusicology, Eastman School of Music
Established 2008, first title forthcoming

Musical Encounters at the 1889 Paris World's Fair
✤ Annegret Fauser

Mendelssohn, Goethe, and the **Walpurgis Night**

John Michael Cooper

THE PLEASURE OF MODERNIST MUSIC

Listening, Meaning, Intention, Ideology

Edited by Arved Ashby

DANE RUDHYAR

HIS MUSIC, THOUGHT, AND ART

DENIZ ERTAN

the substance of things: heard

writings about music

paul griffiths

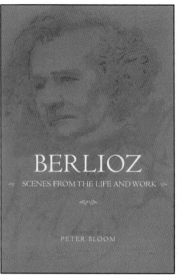

BERLIOZ

SCENES FROM THE LIFE AND WORK

EDITED BY
PETER BLOOM

B·E·R·L·I·O·Z

PAST, PRESENT, FUTURE

Edited by PETER BLOOM

The
Rosary
Cantoral

Ritual and Social Design
in a Chantbook from
Early Renaissance Toledo

Lorenzo Candelaria

MUSICKING
SHAKESPEARE

A
Conflict
of
Theatres

Daniel
Albright

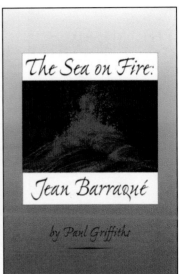

The Sea on Fire:

Jean Barraqué

by Paul Griffiths

SCHUBERT
IN·THE·EUROPEAN
IMAGINATION

VOLUME I: THE ROMANTIC AND VICTORIAN ERAS

SCOTT MESSING

EDITED BY PETER DICKINSON

Cage Talk

Dialogues
With & About
John Cage

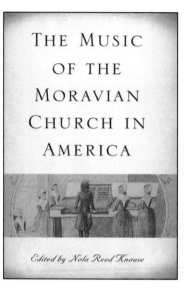

THE MUSIC
OF THE
MORAVIAN
CHURCH IN
AMERICA

Edited by Nola Reed Knouse

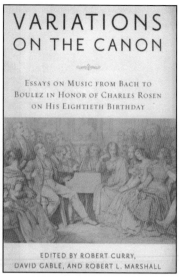

VARIATIONS
ON THE CANON

Essays on Music from Bach to
Boulez in Honor of Charles Rosen
on His Eightieth Birthday

EDITED BY ROBERT CURRY,
DAVID GABLE, AND ROBERT L. MARSHALL

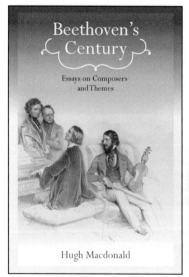

Beethoven's
Century

Essays on Composers
and Themes

Hugh Macdonald

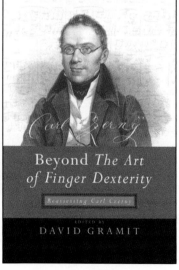

Beyond *The Art
of Finger Dexterity*

Reassessing Carl Czerny

EDITED BY
DAVID GRAMIT

POWER
RELATIONS
IN NIGERIA:
Ilorin Slaves and Their Successors

ANN O'HEAR

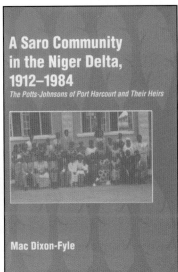

A Saro Community
in the Niger Delta,
1912–1984
The Potts-Johnsons of Port Harcourt and Their Heirs

Mac Dixon-Fyle

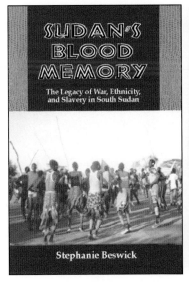

SUDAN'S
BLOOD
MEMORY
The Legacy of War, Ethnicity, and Slavery in South Sudan

Stephanie Beswick

Indirect Rule
in South Africa
Tradition, Modernity, and the
Costuming of Political Power

J. C. Myers

The **URBAN ROOTS OF Democracy AND POLITICAL VIOLENCE IN ZIMBABWE**

HARARE AND HIGHFIELD, 1940–1964

TIMOTHY SCARNECCHIA

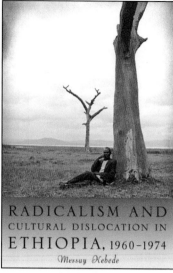

RADICALISM AND CULTURAL DISLOCATION IN ETHIOPIA, 1960–1974

Messay Kebede

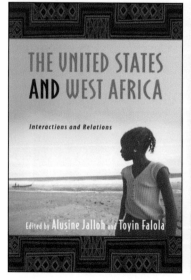

THE UNITED STATES AND WEST AFRICA

Interactions and Relations

Edited by **Alusine Jalloh** and **Toyin Falola**

BEN ENWONWU

THE MAKING OF AN AFRICAN MODERNIST

SYLVESTER OKWUNODU OGBECHIE

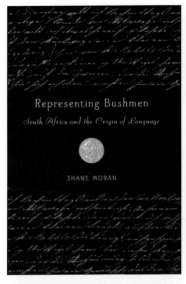

Representing Bushmen

South Africa and the Origin of Language

SHANE MORAN

Afro-Brazilians

CULTURAL PRODUCTION
IN A RACIAL DEMOCRACY

Niyi Afolabi

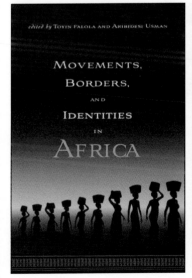

edited by TOYIN FALOLA AND ARIBIDESI USMAN

MOVEMENTS,

BORDERS,

AND

IDENTITIES

IN

AFRICA

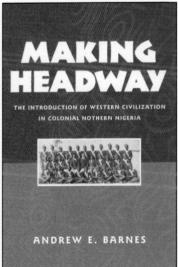

MAKING
HEADWAY

THE INTRODUCTION OF WESTERN CIVILIZATION
IN COLONIAL NOTHERN NIGERIA

ANDREW E. BARNES

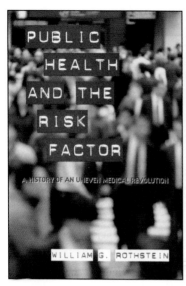

PUBLIC
HEALTH
AND THE
RISK
FACTOR

A HISTORY OF AN UNEVEN MEDICAL REVOLUTION

WILLIAM G. ROTHSTEIN

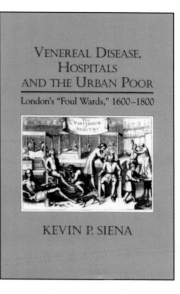

VENEREAL DISEASE,
HOSPITALS
AND THE URBAN POOR

London's "Foul Wards," 1600–1800

KEVIN P. SIENA

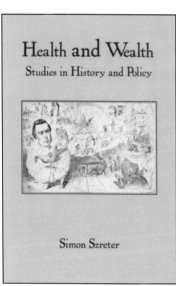

Health and Wealth

Studies in History and Policy

Simon Szreter

CHARLES NICOLLE
PASTEUR'S IMPERIAL MISSIONARY
TYPHUS AND TUNISIA

KIM PELIS

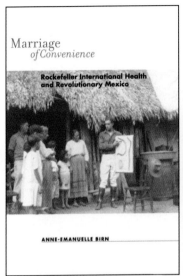

Marriage
of Convenience

**Rockefeller International Health
and Revolutionary Mexico**

ANNE-EMANUELLE BIRN

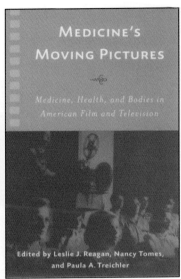

MEDICINE'S
MOVING PICTURES

*Medicine, Health, and Bodies in
American Film and Television*

**Edited by Leslie J. Reagan, Nancy Tomes,
and Paula A. Treichler**

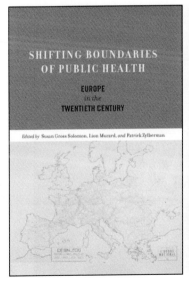

SHIFTING BOUNDARIES
OF PUBLIC HEALTH

EUROPE
in the
TWENTIETH CENTURY

Edited by Susan Gross Solomon, Lion Murard, *and* Patrick Zylberman

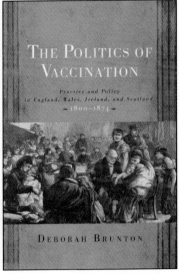

THE POLITICS OF
VACCINATION

*Practice and Policy
in England, Wales, Ireland, and Scotland,
~ 1800–1874 ~*

DEBORAH BRUNTON

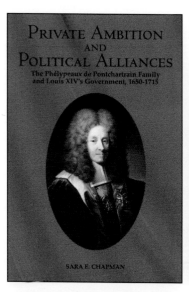

PRIVATE AMBITION
AND
POLITICAL ALLIANCES
The Phélypeaux de Pontchartrain Family
and Louis XIV's Government, 1650-1715

SARA E. CHAPMAN

THE
POLITICS
OF PIETY
FRANCISCAN PREACHERS DURING
THE WARS OF RELIGION, 1560-1600

MEGAN C. ARMSTRONG

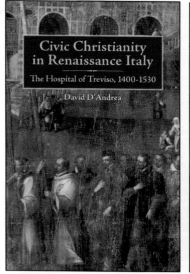

Civic Christianity
in Renaissance Italy
The Hospital of Treviso, 1400-1530

David D'Andrea

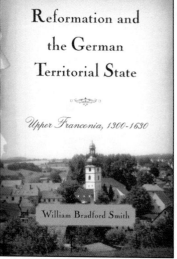

Reformation and
the German
Territorial State

Upper Franconia, 1300-1630

William Bradford Smith

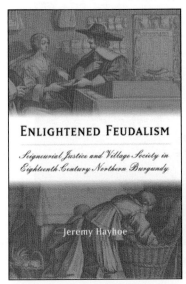

ENLIGHTENED FEUDALISM

Seigneurial Justice and Village Society in Eighteenth-Century Northern Burgundy

Jeremy Hayhoe

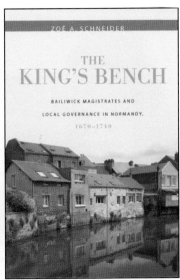

ZOË A. SCHNEIDER

THE
KING'S BENCH

BAILIWICK MAGISTRATES AND

LOCAL GOVERNANCE IN NORMANDY,

1670–1740

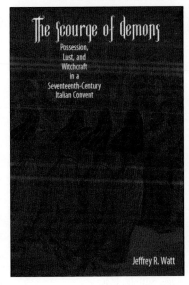

The Scourge of demons

Possession,
Lust, and
Witchcraft
in a
Seventeenth-Century
Italian Convent

Jeffrey R. Watt

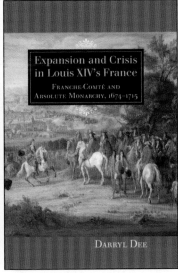

Expansion and Crisis
in Louis XIV's France

FRANCHE-COMTÉ AND
ABSOLUTE MONARCHY, 1674–1715

DARRYL DEE

Home of the University of Rochester Press and Boydell & Brewer Inc. at 668 Mt. Hope Avenue, Rochester, NY. This historic building, part of the University's Mt. Hope Campus, was originally the office building for the Ellwanger and Barry Nurseries.

Current home of Boydell & Brewer Group Ltd. and Boydell & Brewer Ltd. at Whitwell House in Melton near Woodbridge, Suffolk, U.K.

Location, Location, Location

The old adage about real estate is certainly true for the Press. In useful proximity to the provost's office, a very few Press staffers started off in the Administration Building (now Wallis Hall). When more space was required, however, a new location had to be found in order to keep the growing URP and Boydell staff together. Further, it was important to ensure that authors, editors, vendors, board members, and others had easy access. With this in mind, the Press moved to University property at 668 Mt. Hope Avenue in 1995 (see color insert). This building, years ago housing the offices of the Ellwanger and Barry Nursery, is flanked by the University president's house and the provost's house. Initially the Press occupied the first floor of this building and used the basement area for storage and files. As the Press and Boydell & Brewer continued to grow, the operation fully took over 668 Mt. Hope Avenue in 2001. Boydell & Brewer continues to pay rent to the University for the space not devoted to University of Rochester operations.

For a period of time, the Mt. Hope office also housed the Camden House Press editorial director, Jim Walker, although his office was eventually relocated to Elizabethtown, New York. Boydell & Brewer had acquired Camden House Press (whose primary emphasis is on scholarly books dealing with German and Austrian literature) in 1998.

At the time of the agreement with Boydell & Brewer, their offices were located in buildings at Stangrove Hall in Alderton, Woodbridge, Suffolk. In 2004 the company moved its operations to Whitewell House in Melton, Woodbridge (see color insert).

Eastman Studies in Music:
Exploring the Many Facets of an Art and Practice

Ralph P. Locke

Professor of Musicology, Eastman School of Music

Music is a curious field. Nearly everyone loves some kind of music, and some people love many kinds. But, unlike novels or poems or plays or paintings, musical works cannot easily be represented in words or visual images, the two primary communications systems of the book trade. Furthermore, musical notation—the basic way in which the compositions of the great Western tradition are set down, from Gregorian Chant to composers of today such as Steve Reich—feels opaque to many music lovers, even those who attend concerts or opera regularly or have, at some point in life, studied an instrument or sung in a chorus.

The net result has been a looming gap, for several centuries now, between the aspects of music that music professionals take for granted and the ways in which music has tended to be written about in books, magazines, and newspapers. This gap provides academic and other niche publishers with an opportunity, one that the Eastman Studies in Music series has attempted to fill for some eighteen years.

It was in the early 1990s that Robert Easton (URP's first director) and Jürgen Thym (then professor and chair of musicology at the Eastman School of Music) asked me if I would develop a music series for the nascent Press, and I gratefully said yes. I had edited a scholarly journal for a few years, and I had published a monograph based on my dissertation (through University of Chicago Press) and was co-editing a multi-author book (for University of California Press). I thus had some sense of the amount of additional work that editing a book series would probably cause for me (URP had minimal staff in its early years) and of the likely stumbling blocks.

But I was no less aware of the rich possibilities. A healthy university press, I felt, would speak well to the world about the often-hidden merits of the University of Rochester, and a music series—the name, everyone agreed, would be Eastman Studies in Music—would raise awareness more specifically about the high-level work that goes on in the nonperformance departments of the Eastman School of Music. I also urged that the "call for manuscripts" set no constraints on subject matter or methodology. Quality and significance would be paramount. I hated the idea of having to reject a project because it dealt with the "wrong" century, genre, or country, focused heavily on archival fact-collecting (sometimes derided as merely "positivistic"), or relied upon one or another current in music analysis or cultural criticism.

I was also concerned, at least at the outset, that the Eastman Studies series not publish too many writings by Eastman faculty members, lest it appear to be a kind of vanity press. The series, I felt (and still feel), should simply strive to maintain Eastman- and U of R–level standards of excellence, and should use expertise from Eastman and other universities in order to maintain those standards. I put together an editorial advisory board in which the Eastman appointees were slightly outnumbered, as a matter of principle, by outsiders from major research universities. These outsiders included, during the early years, such notable scholars as Charles Hamm (Dartmouth), Bonnie C. Wade (Berkeley), Craig Wright (Yale), and Neal Zaslaw (Cornell). Ellen Koskoff, from Eastman, also served for a time. She has recently initiated a new series for the Press that is more closely defined than Eastman

Studies but, in its own way, still dauntingly broad: Eastman/ Rochester Studies in Ethnomusicology.

Once the reputation of the Eastman Studies series was secure, I began to feel comfortable having a precisely balanced board: three members from Eastman and three from the outside. Two Eastmanites—Gretchen Wheelock (Department of Musicology) and Robert Wason (Music Theory)—have served on the board from the start; for some years now they have been joined by Chair of Musicology Patrick Macey. The three current non-Eastmanites are Sarah Fuller (SUNY-Stony Brook), William Caplin (McGill), and the aforementioned Bonnie Wade.

The first authors to be published in the series were a varied and distinguished lot. Margaret G. Cobb, the *doyenne* of Debussy studies, contributed an urgently needed revised edition of her famous book *The Poetic Debussy.* It went on to sell out in hard cover and paperback alike. (Like many URP books, it is now available again, thanks in part to advances made in the technology of on-demand reprinting.) Joscelyn Godwin's *Music and the Occult: French Musical Philosophies, 1750–1950* likewise made it into paperback. So did the first of several Eastman Studies books on organ music, Lawrence Archbold and William Peterson's *French Organ Music from the Revolution to Franck and Widor.*

Clearly, we realized, our concept was working. And, just as clearly, we were getting—because of my own scholarly proclivities—an overabundance of titles on French topics. We gradually vanquished that problem, with books on such topics as music publishing in sixteenth-century Venice, fugal theory in the Baroque era, Bach, Wagner, "the pleasure of modernist music" (e.g., Schoenberg and Stravinsky), and numerous aspects of music and musical life in the

United States. A distinctly American book, Elliott Carter's *Collected Essays and Lectures,* quickly became one of the Press's all-time best-sellers (in hard cover and paperback) and remains in print today—to the satisfaction, we hope, of the renowned composer, who celebrated his hundredth birthday in December 2008 by attending the first performance of his latest work (a piano concerto) by the Boston Symphony Orchestra.

Some interesting and important manuscripts written by performers did not seem quite right for the series because they tended to take a tone that was less scholarly, even healthfully opinionated. With the eager support of Robert Easton and his successors Sean Culhane, Tim Madigan, and now Suzanne Guiod, I therefore proposed such books as stand-alone items, outside the Eastman Studies series. Again, we seem to have guessed right, as these books sold well, and one of them gained particularly glowing reviews: *The Percussionist's Art: Same Bed, Different Dreams,* by a remarkable West Coast master of multiple percussion, Steven Schick. For that book's front cover we were pleased to find an intriguing (and fee-free) photo of clay flower pots: Schick discusses a musical work that required these "instruments" and explains how he deals with the seemingly inevitable occasion when one of them, in the midst of a performance, is suddenly reduced to shards.

The Press also (in its early days) purchased the back stock of UMI Research Press books on music history and theory, many of them derived from dissertations. Several of these have now appeared in revised editions, bearing a URP imprint (but, because they were already part of another series, not that of Eastman Studies).

Needless to say, as time went along, the board members and I were not able to resist the offer of important manuscripts from some members of the Eastman faculty. These manuscripts are peer reviewed in the usual way, with confidential readings at several stages by specialist scholars at other institutions. Eastman Studies authors who are current or former members of the Eastman School's music theory and musicology departments include Elizabeth West Marvin (co-editor, *Concert Music, Rock, and Jazz since 1960*), Matthew Brown (*Explaining Tonality: Schenkerian Theory and Beyond*), David Beach (*Aspects of Unity in J. S. Bach's Partitas and Suites*), and Kerala J. Snyder (*Dieterich Buxtehude: Organist in Lübeck,* revised edition; its CD contains splendid performances by, among others, Eastman Professor of Organ Hans Davidsson). One forthcoming book, *Of Poetry and Song: Approaches to the Nineteenth-Century Lied,* has connections both to the Eastman School and to the University of Rochester's College of Arts, Sciences, and Engineering. This much-awaited interdisciplinary volume consists of new and classic essays by Jürgen Thym (emeritus, Musicology) and the late Ann C. Fehn (Modern Languages) as well as by two distinguished colleagues from other institutions, Harry E. Seelig (University of Massachusetts–Amherst) and Rufus Hallmark (Rutgers).

A book, like a hill, can be alive with the sound of music. *The Percussionist's Art* contains, tucked into a little pocket, a thrilling compact disc of many of the pieces that Schick discusses in detail. The Press has similarly provided CDs for Eastman Studies books on such topics as Indonesian music (*The Gamelan Digul*), the great Chinese *erhu* player Abing (*Musical Creativity in Twentieth-Century China*), and, most recently, some forgotten but charming, and socially revealing, operettas (*Music in German Immigrant Music Theater: New York City, 1840–1940*). One Eastman Studies title contains not one but two CDs: *Composing with Japanese Instruments,* a practical guide (widely used in its original Japanese version) by the eminent composer Minoru Miki.

At the time of this writing, the Eastman Studies series has released more than sixty titles, and many more are in the pipeline. We are pleased that our books have been so well received in the scholarly world and also in the general press. Excerpts from favorable reviews appearing in *Times Literary Supplement* and *BBC Music Magazine* can be read on the URP website. Particularly heartening was this sentence from a review in *Music and Letters* of Scott Messing's two-volume *Schubert in the European Imagination*: "Offers yet more evidence that the University of Rochester Press has become a highly significant player in the field." The appearance of the series' fiftieth title—*Music Theory and Mathematics*—in February 2008 brought welcome attention to the Press as a whole, as has Boydell's music-book blog entitled *From Beyond the Stave*. (The wordplay is clearer if you pronounce "stave"—the British equivalent of the musical term "staff"—with a long *a*.) See for example an overview of the music books of 2008 at http://frombeyondthestave. blogspot.com/2008/12/our-books-of-year.html. The University's "Eastman Studies at 50" press release was carried at several much-visited sites, including http://www.berkshirereview.net/music/eastman_studies.html.

In addition to receiving favorable reviews, two Eastman Studies books have won awards: *ForeWord Magazine* selected *The Musical Madhouse* (the first English translation of Berlioz's delightful book *Les grotesques de la musique*) as one of its Big Ten Picks from University Presses for 2003, and *Theories of Fugue from the Age of Josquin to the Age of Bach* received the 2002 William H. Scheide Prize (American Bach Society) for a publication of exceptional merit on Bach or figures in his circle. I should also mention that the series' book jackets have gradually, thanks in part to recent lower prices for full-color printing, moved from functional to gorgeous. There was particular acclaim for the cover design of *Musical Encounters at the 1889 Paris World's Fair,* which the Press based on a poster from the period.

As prices rise and libraries and individuals trim back their book purchases, many Eastman Studies books have been helped by a subvention from the author's home institution or a scholarly society. No fewer than seven Eastman Studies books dealing in part or whole with music in the United States have received a welcome boost from the Howard Hanson Institute for American Music: the latest is a two-volume study of the string quartet since 1900, in which American composers John Cage, Elliott Carter, Mel Powell, Milton Babbitt, and Shulamit Ran rightly sit shoulder to shoulder with Debussy, Sibelius, Bartók, Schoenberg, and Shostakovich.

Challenges remain, of course. The book-with-CD looks likely to be replaced by the book-with-audio-files-on-a-website. But, regardless of shifts in technology and funding, Eastman Studies aims to remain a major purveyor of serious—and, in many cases, also brightly engaging—discussion of music for the specialist and the general reader alike. We do not hesitate to include musical examples and sometimes even provide them in abundance. Still, certain books do not need examples and restrict themselves (wonderfully) to words alone: for example, renowned music critic Paul Griffiths's exquisitely edited collection of some of his most fascinating reviews and essays, *The Substance of Things Heard.* I can only thank the boards of the University of Rochester Press and of Boydell & Brewer for sensing the need for high-level books on music and realizing that a series run by a team of scholars (and supported now by a great editorial and production staff!) could meet that need.

৵৹

Rochester Studies in African History and the Diaspora

By Toyin Falola
Frances Higginbotham Nalle Centennial
Professor in History, University of Texas at Austin

I proposed the idea to establish the series in 1995 after editorial director Sean M. Culhane requested that I evaluate a manuscript on Africa he had received. As part of my report, I told him that publishing the book as a stand alone, while a good idea, had to confront the difficulty of marketing. The Press could not take just one title to display at conferences, nor would it be sufficient for a catalogue. A body of titles, I argued, was necessary, but it must be structured and defined to have coherence. To establish a series, I pointed out, they needed a series editor to scout for manuscripts, relate unsolicited ones to the series focus, evaluate them, and submit reports to the editorial board for approval. A series would be much easier to sell to libraries, and there was the possibility of co-publishing with presses in other countries. I was also able to persuade Culhane that publishing on diverse issues without a focused series would weaken all the volumes. Marketing each new book would be frustrating.

Culhane, a meticulous editor, saw the sense in my point of view and asked for my suggestions. At that time, Indiana, Heinemann, Cambridge, Oxford, James Currey, Ohio, Westview, and Lynne Rienner all had established series on Africa. To compete with these and others we needed an original focus, one that anticipated a new generation of scholars and readers.

The focus on Africa and the African diaspora, as well as the orientation of the series, was arrived at by the historical circumstances of the 1990s, specifically, the changing nature of African history and the depressing conditions of the 1990s. The field of African history was created in the 1940s, and it expanded rather quickly by the 1960s. By the 1990s, however, there were deep concerns regarding its continued success. The publication of monographs was undergoing a serious recession; all leading series established in Africa and published abroad, notably the Ibadan History Series and the Legon History Series, both by Longman, had collapsed. Heinemann had already announced that it would terminate the publication of its prestigious African Writers' Series. Greenwood was later to buy Heinemann, and further de-emphasize its interest in Africa.

Further, the academic and political contexts of the 1990s reflected some of the tensions and challenges of the post–Cold War era. The barriers between Africa and the rest of the world appeared to be widening, leading communication and exchange of ideas to become increasingly difficult. And the resurgence of ethnic nationalism in Eastern Europe and the creation of millions of refugees in Europe and Africa meant that we had to rethink previous academic assumptions on a wide range of issues, not the least identity, race, nationalism, and ethnicity. Africa experienced increased marginalization as

Eastern Europe and the Middle East acquired the limelight, with significant implications for the production of knowledge that shaped the general orientation of the series. Many local journals in Africa perished, and many journals and monographs devoted to Africa in other parts of the world witnessed some sort of decline. Obtaining institutional support, persuading excellent scholars to serve as editors, and acquiring original monographs became great obstacles.

Publishers turned their attention elsewhere as the African book market became unattractive. Western scholars stopped publishing in Africa, and Africans who wanted to publish in the West encountered serious challenges as the general unavailability of current materials diminished the quality of their contributions. Thus, part of the challenge of the series was to overcome the barrier by representing African voices. When we published Adiele Afigbo's *The Abolition of the Slave Trade in Southeastern Nigeria, 1885–1950,* we became the first major series in the U.S. to publish the work of a scholar based in Africa. Later, the series published *Representing Bushmen: South Africa and the Origin of Language,* by Shane Moran of South Africa, which offers convincing evidence that perhaps no African tradition remains so oversimplified within popular history as those of Southern Africa's San people (aka Bushmen). To this day, Rochester remains at the forefront by bringing Africa-based voices to the mainstream academy.

The 1990s were also a time of intensified globalization, with major impact on African societies, economies, and politics. African scholars were relocating to the West in large numbers, creating new transnational communities, and inserting themselves into the American academy. Although Africa remained remote and exotic, transnationalists joined established constituencies to bring Africa closer to home. The series merges these issues of location, diversity, difference, and the commonalities in global humanities. Issues relating to events and the human values that shape them are neither homogenized nor presented in dogmatic or absolute terms. Neither do the volumes present academic issues as advocacy, even when they touch upon race, class, and identity.

In this context, the series recognizes the need to extend the frontiers of knowledge about Africa and the African diaspora, without contributing to polarizations, stereotypes, and ethnocentricities. In July 1995, I offered a broad description that states:

> With contributions from both emerging and established scholars and reflecting a variety of perspectives and approaches, this series is about Africa writ large and its diasporic extensions. Each book will be insightful, broadly comprehensive and based on rich evidence. As much as possible, every work that is included must demonstrate relevance to Africa, either by the theme that is explored or connections with broad theoretical literature. The series will consciously encourage studies that are located within the context of debates internal to Africa and those generated by the exciting and growing field of African studies in the West, in order to further an understanding of the key challenges facing Africa in the 21st century as well as the sacrifices and contribution of Africans to the development of the modern world. As a general principle, each manuscript must contribute to a clearer understanding of at least some aspects of the many issues that currently confront Africans of the continent and those of the diaspora.

I specified three aspects of newness:

> To be especially encouraged are manuscripts focused on economic history, which will build up the kind of literature that helps to make more intelligible the current economic problems of continental Africans and Africans of the diaspora. Also to be encouraged are such new themes as cultural, comparative, and environmental history. As there are various categories that are misunderstood because they are investigated in isolation, studies that deal with the intersections between different categories of knowledge will be given preference.

I closed by emphasizing what the key contributions of the series would be:

- The series will address issues on the cutting edge, generating and contributing to key debates in African studies. The development of property rights and other socioeconomic and political institutions, in the context of economic development processes—at local, regional, national or continental levels—are expected to be central themes. Identity, gender, culture and race are also new "growth areas" that have yet to be covered in existing books. There are other significant historical and theoretical themes not often discussed with regard to African history such as subaltern and cultural studies and literary criticism.
- The series will bridge the gap between Africa and the African diaspora, the first to make this connection. Diaspora is broadly defined to include manuscripts on the Americas, Europe, Islam, and Indian Ocean history as these connect with Africa.

- Existing series are deliberately geared to satisfy the needs and pedagogies of a small circle of North African and European scholars. This has tended to generate a void in scholarship that underprivileges alternative voices and narrows the perspectives for understanding Africa. The Rochester series will accommodate diverse methodologies and perspectives of Africa and the diaspora.

- As most existing series ignore the modern period of Africa, this is an area that will receive prominence, as the continent moves into a new century, with the need to meet the expectations of a new generation of students and public.

Thus from the onset, we defined the mission in broad terms to cover historical and contemporary experience in all its ramifications and manifestations: cultural, institutional, economic, and social. Some volumes have dealt with the complexity of encounters with the West (as in slavery and colonialism, tracking the nature of domination and its legacy), as well as race relations within specific countries, as in the recent book by Niyi Afolabi, *Afro-Brazilians: Cultural Production in a Racial Democracy.*

The series created an immediate impact. Its founding symbolized the expansion of African history as a discipline and its infusion with the African diaspora broadly defined. The series has featured the most prominent and renowned scholars of African studies, and has promoted younger scholars whose work has (and will continue to) shape the field. In addition, it is unique in publishing competing groups and contending visions of African studies, from the "African perspective" to "Afrocentric."

Thus far, the series has covered all historical eras, from the precolonial to the present, in countries such as Algeria, Angola, Brazil, Cuba, Equatorial Africa, Gambia, Germany, Ghana, Kenya, Liberia, Malawi, Mauritius, Mozambique, Namibia, Nigeria, Senegal, Sierra Leone, South Africa, Sudan, Togo, and Zimbabwe.

Professor Olufemi Vaughan, the Geoffrey Canada Professor of History & Africana Studies and Director, Africana Studies Program, Bowdoin College, and author of *Nigerian Cheifs: Traditional Power in Modern Politics, 1890s-1990s,* published by the Press in 2000, offers an author's perspective on the series:

"Established at a time when the older university and academic presses were closing down their series in African studies because of the economic crisis that engulfed the continent in the 1980s, Professor Falola was able to parlay his enormous reputation to encourage the establishment of what would quickly become one the most respected and authoritative series in African studies. Widely known for its profound range of themes and depth of academic rigor and erudition, I will underscore the issues that I believe sets Rochester Studies in History and the Diaspora apart from its competitors, namely Cambridge, Clarendon (Oxford), Indiana, Wisconsin, and Edinburgh.

"First, Rochester is the first Africanist series that seriously engaged the study of Africa on its own terms, eschewing the penchant of these older series to favor prevailing Western paradigms in the social sciences and humanities. In this context, the Rochester series substituted such Western paradigmatic preoccupations with intellectual rigor, strong and clear analytical and writing skills, systematic presentation of relevant facts, argumentation, and dogged primary and secondary research.

"Second, despite its emphasis on historical studies, Rochester welcomed innovative and original scholarship that underscored distinctive interdisciplinary perspectives and critical intellectual and theoretical reflection in the humanities and social sciences. This perspective favored Africanist scholarship and research that engaged dynamic African experiences in a complex world.

"Third, Rochester was the first of the very best African series to transcend the conventional colonial boundaries of the older series. For the first time African studies was not trapped in colonial and postcolonial straightjackets that inhibit dynamic articulations of the African experience. African historical studies now could incorporate dynamic diasporic and transnational encounters between African societies in any given region, while engaging the experiences of African peoples across the great water ways of the Atlantic in the context of modernity.

"Fourth, Rochester welcomed studies that engage local African knowledge production with Western philosophic and epistemological perspectives—the first of its kind among the leading African studies series.

"Fifth, Rochester opened its doors to both established Africanists and took chances with emerging scholars whose rigorous works were raising new and fresh questions that were transforming the field. In this context, Rochester pioneered and legitimated the outstanding works of a new generation of African scholars who had no pedigree and no connection to the powerful Western scholars who dominated the older African studies presses.

"Finally, Rochester envisioned an African studies series that integrated innovative epistemological, theoretical, and analytical perspective with the real aspirations and conditions of African peoples and peoples of African ancestry through-out the world. This has contributed to what has now become Africana studies—the integration of African studies and African diaspora studies in leading Western universities in the world, especially in the United States."

The series remains competitive in what it does best: publish books that merge cultural studies and history. We encourage people in Africa to publish with us, and we also highlight the interactions between continental and dia-sporic scholarship. The books in the RSAHD series reflect the characteristics of a new generation of African scholar-ship in subject, theory, and representation. We support the work of younger scholars doing innovative work on gender, development, democratization, political reform, inclusion of multiple constituencies, tracing precolonial history, under-standing the impact of colonialism, agency in globalization, and much more. The annual conference on Africa that I convene at the University of Texas at Austin has enabled us to remain a step ahead of our competitors in addressing cur-rent and major issues in African studies. Each year, from a range of over a hundred essays, we are able to publish a selection of the best in an edited volume, thereby announc-ing through the series products of new research and helping to build the careers of the next generation of Africanists.

The series has become an inevitable companion for scholars of Africa, especially in the humanities and social sciences. Its versatile and wide-ranging coverage of issues rank it as one of the favored places for scholars to obtain insightful and up-to-date information and material both for research and teaching in the field of African studies. The series provides bridges between Africa and the rest of the world in various significant ways. It is not merely an outlet for scholars with interest in issues internal to Africa; rather, it is has attracted scholars of quality with active research on Africa across the globe. The inclusion of the diaspora provides a unique exposition of Africa and African issues, wherever they may be found. The series provides explication of complex issues beyond the mere documentation of facts; as such, it is as theoretically grounded as it is data driven. There has been no dogmatic view or school of thought noticeable in the series as a result of an open-minded approach that is driven by knowledge and the advancement of scholarship rather than by ideology. As a result, it has provided opportunities for lively debate on Africa and the rest of the world. Historical and contemporary issues find careful examination based on leading views and theories. The series has presented a wider framework that subsumes different voices and perspectives on African discourse as it has generated topics for conferences that invariably have informed further publications and research.

The books in the series represent a fitting symbol of the strengths of Africa and the African diaspora as disciplines. Some have done well, encouraging us to reprint them in paperback. A few have made it to the classroom as textbooks, while others have received awards. Our authors have continued to distinguish themselves, many on the basis of our books, as in the case of Kwaku Korang who became editor of the leading journal in his field, *Research in African Literatures;* Nemata Blyden, whom we published as a young assistant professor, is now the director of the Africana Studies Program at George Washington University; Joshua Forrest has become a notable intellectual figure; and Alusine Jalloh is director of the Africa Program at the University of Texas at Arlington. We have also published the works of the most famous and established scholars in the field, as in the case of Ben Lindfors and Crawford Young.

We remain committed to a broadly defined but manageable series. The combination of the ideas in our founding documents, the rate of manuscript submission, and the collection from the annual Austin conference will sustain the series into the future. As the modern history of Africa is written, the series aims to occupy a major chapter in it.

Rochester Studies in Central Europe

The Press's book series in Central European Studies began in 2000 under the direction of Ewa Hauser, director of the University of Rochester's Skalny Center for Polish and Central European Studies from its inception in 1994 until 2007, and a senior associate in the University's political science department. In 2008, the series was recast and its focus broadened to invite works that cross traditional disciplinary, geographic, and period boundaries. The current series editor is Timothy Snyder, history professor at Yale University, frequent contributor to *New York Review of Books, Times Literary Supplement*, and *The Nation*; and author of the acclaimed book, *The Reconstruction of Nations: Poland, Ukraine, Lithuania, Belarus, 1569–1999* (Yale University Press, 2003), and several other volumes on the history of East Europe. A board of editorial advisors with diverse areas of expertise assists the series by recommending projects and consulting on proposals. Current publications include contemporary and historical works on topics related to the region's culture and history—comparative politics, religion, film and media, urban and gender studies. Titles published to date:

Post-Communist Tradition: The Thorny Road by former Polish finance minister Grzegorz W. Kolodko (2000)

The Polish Formalist School and Russian Formalism by Andrzej Karcz (2002, in cooperation with the Jagiellonian University Press)

Globalization and Catching-Up in Transition Economies by Grzegorz W. Kolodko (2002)

Music in the Culture of Polish Galicia, 1772-1914 by Jolanta T. Pekacz (2002)

Ideology, Politics, and Diplomacy in East Central Europe edited by M.B.B. Biskupski (2003)

Between East and West: Polish and Russian Nineteenth-Century Travel to the Orient by Izabela Kalinowska (2004)

The Polish Singers Alliance of American 1888-1998: Choral Patriotism by Stanlislaus A. Blejwas (2005)

A Clean Sweep? The Politics of Ethnic Cleansing in Western Poland, 1945-1960 by T. David Curp (2006)

စာ

Rochester Studies in Philosophy

The Rochester Studies in Philosophy series was started under the editorship of Wade L. Robison, Ezra Hale Professor in Applied Ethics at the Rochester Institute of Technology. His series board sought "a mix of titles and formats, ranging from monographs by a single author to edited volumes representing many authors and points of view. . . . The focus of the series is on eighteenth- and nineteenth-century philosophy, especially the work and influence of such figures as Spinoza, Leibnitz, Berkeley, Hume, Kant, and Nietzsche."

In 2000, the Rochester Studies in Philosophy series published *The Scottish Enlightenment: Essays in Reinterpretation* edited by Paul Wood. This was a collection of ten commissioned essays on five themes central to the Scottish Enlightenment, exploring its relationship to the European Enlightenment. The *Bulletin for the History of Medicine* called it a "splendid collection . . . it offers a set of essays that each stands on its own but when taken together provide a superb exposition of leading themes in the study of the Scottish Enlightenment over the past few decades."

This was followed by *Kant's Legacy: Essays in Honor of Lewis White Beck* edited by Predrag Cicovacki (2001), honoring a University of Rochester professor who was one of the world's leading Kant scholars. Later titles included *Plato's Erotic Thought: The Tree of the Unknown* by Alfred Geier (2002), also of the University of Rochester faculty, which explored the nature of the object of Eros in Plato's writings; *Leibniz on Purely Extrinsic Denominations* by Dennis Plaisted (2002); *Rationality and Happiness: From the Ancients to the Early Medievals: From the Ancients to the Early Medievals* edited by Jiyuan Yu and Jorge Gracia (2003); *A History of Reasonableness: Testimony and Authority in the Art of Thinking* by Rick Kennedy (2004); and *State of Nature or Eden? Thomas Hobbes and His Contemporaries on the Natural Condition of Human Beings* by Helen Thornton (2005). Six titles were subsequently published:

Fire in the Dark: Essays on Pascal's Pensées and Provinciales by Charles M. Natoli (2005)

Destined for Evil? The Twentieth-Century Reponses edited by Predrag Cicovacki (2005)

David Hume and Eighteenth-Century America by Mark G. Spencer (2005)

Nietzsche's Anthropic Circle: Man, Science, and Myth by George J. Stack (2005)

Religion and the Origins of the German Enlightenment: Faith and the Reform of Learning in the Thought of Christian Thomasius by Thomas Ahnert (2006)

The fourteenth (and last) title published in this series was *The Works of Bishop Butler* edited by David E. White (2006). The work included Butler's complete works in the first newly edited version to appear in a century, and was the only work to include a single, analytic index to the whole works.

∽

Rochester Studies in Medical History

Theodore M. Brown
Professor of History (College of Arts, Sciences, and Engineering) and of Community and Preventive Medicine (School of Medicine and Dentistry), University of Rochester

The Rochester Studies in Medical History series began as the result of a conversation I had over lunch with Sean Culhane, the editor for the Press at that time. In response to his questions, I described the professional field of medical history and the importance of the American Association for the History of Medicine. During our discussion I was able to express my feelings about the need to understand and appreciate the scholarly sophistication and seriousness of the history of medicine as a field. My reward for this altruistic gesture was an invitation to head a new scholarly series—Rochester Studies in Medical History—in an excellent illustration of the maxim that "no good deed goes unpunished."

Within the next year, the series was launched, Tim Madigan became the Press's editorial director, and I was officially designated the senior editor of Rochester Studies in Medical History. Tim already had a first candidate for the series, Marjorie Grene's translation from the German of Thomas Fuchs's *The Mechanization of the Heart: Harvey and Descartes.* Tim was enthusiastic because, as a philosopher, he knew and respected Grene's work in the history of philosophy and thought the study was of interest. I had worked in the area of seventeenth century medical science some decades earlier, knew both Harvey and Descartes scholarship quite well, and, with some assurance, told Tim that the monograph was solid. Thus we had the first volume for the new series.

At this point, I decided to get serious. I invited several respected colleagues in the history of medicine to join me in the venture and to serve as members of an informal but soon-to-be-public advisory board. They were Elizabeth Fee (head of the Medical History Division of the National Library of Medicine), Judith Leavitt (now Ruth Bleier Professor and Rupple Bascom Chair of Medical History and Bioethics at the University of Wisconsin), and David Rosner (now Ronald H. Lauterstein Professor of Sociomedical

Sciences and professor of history at Columbia University). A year or so later, I added three others to the advisory board: Susan Lederer (then at Yale but now Robert Turrell Professor of Medical History and Bioethics at the University of Wisconsin), Michael Sappol (historian in the Medical History Division of the National Library of Medicine), and George Weisz (the Cotton-Hannah Chair of the History of Medicine in the Department of the Social Studies of Medicine at McGill University). We drew up an announcement for the series that was published in the *Bulletin of the History of Medicine,* and inquiries and manuscripts began to come in. I responded to most of the inquiries and did the preliminary evaluation of manuscripts myself, although I did call upon advisory committee members to help me sort through particular cases or to provide recommendations of external reviewers and other advice. We also soon evolved a tradition of having round-robin email exchanges and a breakfast meeting at the annual meeting of the AAHM. We used these meetings to review the status of the series, resolve thorny issues, and brainstorm about possible authors and manuscripts to recruit for the series. We also kept a collective watch on up-and-coming graduate students whose work at the dissertation level seemed promising and perhaps soon publishable.

Over the next few years, the series slowly gained visibility and a solid reputation. We published one volume each in 2002, 2003, and 2004, then two each in 2005, 2006, and 2007. In 2008, we published three volumes and are hoping to maintain at least that pace as we move ahead. Three of our books have proved popular enough to merit re-publication in paperback: William Rothstein's *Public Health and the Risk Factor* (2003 and 2007), Simon Szreter's *Health and Wealth:*

Studies in History and Policy (2005 and 2007), and Leslie Reagan et al.'s *Medicine's Moving Pictures* (2007 and 2008). Our authors are a mix of younger scholars (Kevin Siena, *Venereal Diseases, Hospitals and the Urban Poor* [2004], Kim Pelis, *Charles Nicolle: Pasteur's Imperial Missionary* [2006], and Anne-Emanuelle Birn, *Marriage of Convenience: Rockefeller International Health and Revolutionary Mexico* [2006]) and very well-established and internationally respected ones (Christopher Lawrence, *Rockefeller Money, The Laboratory, and Medicine in Edinburgh, 1919–1930* [2005], Marcos Cueto, *The Value of Health: A History of the Pan American Health Organization* [2008], and Susan Gross Solomon et al., *Shifting Boundaries of Public Health: Europe in the Twentieth Century* [2008]). Our books overall have been reviewed very well in the best scholarly journals and our series has been praised both for substantive solidity and for its production values. One of our books, William Rothstein's *Public Health and the Risk Factor,* was nominated for the 2009 William Henry Welch Medal of the AAHM, an award of great prestige for works of "outstanding scholarly merit in the field of medical history published during the five calendar years preceding the award." Merely to be nominated for this award is a recognition of the highest order.

Scholarly notices from the journals include the following:

On *Venereal Disease, Hospitals and the Urban Poor:* "Kevin Siena has written an insightful book about people who were twice down on their luck in early modern London: poor and poxed. . . . It is a pleasure to read a book so deeply grounded in archival work; Siena's extensive research offers new perspectives on health care in early modern England."

On *Rockefeller Money, the Laboratory, and Medicine in Edinburgh 1919–1930:* "Lawrence's inquiry is a tightly-focused case study. At the same time, he offers as background a panoramic view of the profound changes to medical education and practice between the world wars. . . . Historians of Scotland as well as scholars of modern science and medicine will find much to admire and appreciate in this erudite book."

On *Charles Nicolle, Pasteur's Imperial Missionary:* "Passionate, lucidly written, and carefully researched, Pelis' history of Nobel Prize-winning bacteriologist Dr. Charles Nicolle and his tenure at the Pasteur Institute in Tunis (1903–36) reveals the global nature of Pasteurian medicine and its role in French colonialism. . . . Pelis makes a significant contribution to the history of medicine with humor, clarity, and exhaustive research."

On *Marriage of Convenience: Rockefeller International Health and Revolutionary Mexico:* "In this sophisticated account of seduction, romance, marriage, and separation—international health-style—Anne-Emanuelle Birn delivers a nuanced analysis of the relationship between the Rockefeller Foundation's International Health Division and the revolutionary Mexican government's Departamento de Salubridad Publica over a thirty-year period. . . . Birn expertly weaves the story of public health in Mexico, and the role played by the Rockefeller Foundation in shaping it, into the larger history of revolutionary Mexican politics and reform efforts. . . . [Her] analysis is always focused, and she consistently shows the reader the connections between high politics and the day-to-day undertaking of public health."

Rochester Studies in Medical History has already earned a respected place in the history of medicine and in the larger world of historical scholarship. It does the University of Rochester proud, and its luster is likely to increase in the future.

৵৹

Changing Perspectives on Early Modern Europe

Jim Collins
Professor of History, Georgetown University

In the late 1990s, James Collins, a professor of history at Georgetown University, read that the University of Rochester sought to enhance its emphasis on the humanities to complement its focus on the hard sciences and medicine. At the same time, Cambridge University Press decided to end its long-running series, Studies in Early Modern Europe, and replace it with New Studies in European History. Collins, an editor of the new Cambridge series, was also an alumnus ('71) of University of Rochester.

The third piece of the puzzle fell into place in the summer of 2000, when one of Collins' former PhD students, Sara Chapman, asked if they could review her dissertation, with a view to suggested changes for publication. Word soon spread, and some of Sara's friends asked to come along: first, Megan Armstrong, then Sara Beam, then a group of others—Michael Breen, Hilary Bernstein, and Greg Brown. As the process spun out of control, Collins turned to an old friend, Professor Mack Holt of George Mason University. Together, the two of them hatched the idea of a weekend seminar, at which all present would read the six dissertations and offer comments on how to make each manuscript into a book. The seminar took place at Georgetown in July 2000; Sara Beam could not attend for family reasons, so it dealt with five dissertations.

The seminar went beautifully, except for one problem: neither Holt nor Collins, both of whom had published monographs in the old Cambridge series, could easily cite a publisher who had any special interest in early modern Continental European history. In later discussions, Collins brought up the U of R's desire to emphasize the humanities, and the two of them agreed to try the University of Rochester Press. Collins went to the 2002 annual meeting of the American Historical Association, hoping to talk with the Press. Boydell & Brewer's representative Susan Dykstra-Poel spoke with him, and passed along the name of Timothy Madigan, then editorial director of the Press. A brief inquiry to Madigan got this response (16 January 2002):

> My colleague Susan Dykstra-Poel has shared with me the conversation you both had at the AHA and your e-mail to her yesterday following up on this. We are both very interested in your proposed series idea. Did you see the article in the current *Chronicle of Higher Education* describing the plight of first-time authors getting their manuscripts evaluated and accepted for publication? If not, I can send you a copy by e-mail.... Your proposed series would be an excellent way of addressing this.... The University of Rochester Press is having a board meeting on Monday, January 21st and it would be good if I could alert the board at this time to the possibility of launching such a series.

A flurry of e-mails led to the original series proposal, on January 28, 2002:

Changing Perspectives on Early Modern Europe brings forward the latest research on Europe during the transformation from the medieval to the modern world. The series seeks to publish innovative scholarship on the full range of topical and geographic fields. Moving beyond the religious focus of some existing series, Changing Perspectives will include monographs on cultural, economic, intellectual, political, religious, and social history. We want to publish the finest new scholarship on life within given political units, on inter-cultural exchanges, and on the global dimensions of European development.

The recent disappearance of long-established publishing venues for scholarship on early modern Europe has left an enormous void in the heart of the historiography of Europe. Changing Perspectives on Early Modern Europe offers young scholars working in this area the opportunity to be part of what we believe will quickly become the leading series in the field. One of our goals is to seek out the finest first books by young scholars.

The next step was to appoint an editorial board, and there Mack Holt took the lead. Everyone Mack approached responded with enthusiasm. In short order, the board included an array of distinguished scholars, many of them alumni of the Cambridge series: Karin Friedrich (east central Europe, School of Slavonic Studies, University of London); Robert Frost (east central Europe, Kings College, University of London); Martha Howell (Low Countries, Columbia University); Sara T. Nalle (Spain; William Paterson University); and Dennis Romano (Italy, Syracuse University), as well as Professors Collins and Holt (France). On February 20, Tim Madigan sent an email with official approval from the Press editorial board, and suggesting that we make an official announcement at the meeting of the Society for French Historical Studies, held that April in Toronto. The call for manuscripts reprised some of the initial description, but Mack Holt suggested an important revision: that the series editors would seek out good, first books by younger scholars, given the fact that so many university presses had opted to stop publishing revised dissertations.

The first manuscripts were not long in coming: Megan Armstrong's work on the Franciscans of Paris in the late sixteenth century, and Sara Chapman's Pontchartrain manuscript. Those two books got the series off to a successful start, and completed the circle begun with the 2000 seminar. The series later published a third of the manuscripts, by Michael Breen.

The premise of the series quickly proved accurate, as we were deluged with proposals in the first two or three years. Holt and Collins turned down most of them at the proposal stage. Those manuscripts sent out to readers found a rigorous process: half of all the manuscripts sent to reviewers got turned down between 2002 and 2008. In the early years, in part due to the logjam of unpublished early modern manuscripts, the series received so many proposals that it had to turn down nearly 75 percent of what the editors received.

At the Press, Tim Madigan left in 2004, to be replaced by Suzanne Guiod, who has shepherded the series for most of its existence. That it requires shepherding is evident from the e-mail count (well over one thousand at last check, just counting the inbox). Throughout the process, the staff at the Press have worked closely with the series editors and with designers to create some outstanding books, both intellectually and aesthetically.

Throughout its existence, Changing Perspectives on Early Modern Europe has received remarkable cooperation from scholars in the field. All members of the original editorial advisory board are still in the group. Requests to review manuscripts have almost universally been accepted. Stuart Carroll, in his review of Megan Armstrong's book for *English Historical Review,* made a point of praising the series, and stressing its importance to the field:

"Rochester University Press's [*sic*] attractively produced new series Changing Perspectives on Early Modern Europe is off to a strong start, and the editors, James Collins and Mack Holt, are to be congratulated on a venture which aims to promote the latest research by younger scholars."

The series has accomplished its early goal of providing outstanding young scholars with a venue for quality work. These books began as dissertations at leading universities, such as Brown, Cornell, Emory, Georgetown, Maryland, Princeton, Toronto, and Virginia. Eight of the series' authors have obtained promotion and tenure, in part, on the basis on their book. The series has attracted work from senior scholars such as Jeffrey Watt, Randolph Head, and J. B. Owens. Its reach also extends across international borders: three of its authors are Canadian, teaching at Canadian universities, and it has ongoing inquiries from several scholars in the United Kingdom.

With a much-anticipated book from Darryl Dee in press and some interesting projects in the pipeline, Changing Perspectives on Early Modern Europe expects to build on this success to cement its place as the leading university press series on early modern European history.

&

Gender and Race in America History

In 2008, the University of Rochester Press announced the formation of a new series, Gender and Race in American History, led by series editors Alison Parker of SUNY Brockport and Carol Faulkner of Syracuse University. Inspired by the rich history of political and social activism in New York state, the series will publish books that focus on research at the intersections of gender, race, politics, and reform in American history. The series will work in collaboration with the University of Rochester's Susan B. Anthony Institute and Frederick Douglass Institute to sponsor seminars, lectures, and public speaker series in an effort to identify promising new scholarship and promote books in the series. The first volume in this series is scheduled to publish in 2010.

కరా

Eastman/Rochester Studies in Ethnomusicology

In 2008, a new series, Eastman/Rochester Studies in Ethnomusicology, was established by Eastman School of Music professor of ethnomusicology Ellen Koskoff. This series will publish books on all aspects of music in contemporary world cultures, primarily based on the anthropological method of ethnographic fieldwork, and will examine the intersections between contemporary musical practices of all kinds and their social and cultural contexts. The series aims in particular to showcase studies that illuminate the relationship between music, gender, and sexuality, and will support ancillary materials such as audio files, DVDs, and web-based content to complement the books. Led by Koskoff, the series advisory board is composed of notable scholars from a variety of institutions.

chapter 6

Meliora: An Imprint for the University

W HILE THE MAJOR THRUST OF THE PRESS is to publish high quality scholarly books in select disciplinary areas, there are, from time to time, other books that need to be published specifically for and about the greater University community. That need gave rise to a unique imprint called Meliora Press.

Imprint Forerunners

Before the Meliora imprint was established, the Press indeed took on the task of publishing a number of books that celebrated major anniversaries of the University and some of its significant components—schools, colleges, departments, or special programs. For example, a volume that celebrated the University's one hundred and fiftieth anniversary was *Transforming Ideas: Selected Profiles in University of Rochester Research and Scholarship,* edited by Robert Kraus and Charles E. Phelps (2000). The concluding paragraph of Provost Phelps's preface describes this book and its motivation:

> This collection of essays provides some exciting examples of the types of transforming work that have taken place at the University of Rochester through its first 150

years. Obviously, these essays do not include *every* major idea and invention arising from the University, but they do represent a sampling of the cornucopia of great ideas that the University has become. In reading these essays, all students, alumni, faculty and staff (past and present), the leaders of the University, and the donors who have helped to facilitate this work with their generous and vital contributions can take immense pride and pleasure in being part of this wonderful process.

In the same year as the University's sesquicentennial, the medical center was celebrating seventy-five years of achievement. A commemorative volume, *The University of Rochester Medical Center: Teaching, Discovering, Caring,* edited by Jules Cohen and Robert J. Joynt, was dedicated to "the faculty, staff, students, and alumni of the School of Medicine and Dentistry, the School of Nursing, Strong Memorial Hospital, and our affiliated hospitals, who have inspired and brought about the achievements described in this book—and have made the University of Rochester Medical Center a beloved and respected institution." Both volumes were distributed by the University to their various worldwide constituencies.

Several similar titles by University of Rochester faculty authors were also in production:

In *An Englishman's Journey along America's Eastern Waterways: The 1831 Illustrated Journal of Herbert Holtham's Travels* (2001), editor Seymour I. Schwartz (author of *Mismapping America,* described earlier) reproduced a version of the handwritten diary of a Unitarian minister from Brighton, England, who came to the United States in the spring of 1831 and spent several months traveling in the Northeast. The diary also contained a number of sketches made along his journey, including several of the Rochester environs. The diary was published in conjunction with the Rochester Museum and Science Center.

Rain of Years: Great Expectations and the World of Dickens by Bernard N. Schilling (2001) was the noted English scholar's last book. A compact survey of all of the novels by Charles Dickens, it was published in cooperation with the Friends of Rush Rhees Library.

Neurology and Neurosurgery: Basic Principles by Frank P. Smith (2002) was written to merge neurological and neurosurgical principles and practice, for improved patient care. The book was published in cooperation with the University of Rochester Medical Center.

The extent and institutional importance of these publications led the Press to establish a special imprint for such books that would differentiate them from the core list of scholarly, peer-reviewed books that formed the mainstay of Press publications.

Meliora!

The choice of name for the new imprint on University-related topics was a natural one: "Meliora" is the motto of the University, connoting the meaning "ever better." The imprint now includes:

Resonance: A History of the University of Rochester Electrical Engineering Department by Edwin Kinnen (2002)

Paul Yu Remembered: The Life and Work of a Distinguished Cardiologist by Jules Cohen and Stephanie Brown Clark (2003)

A Jewel in the Crown: Essays in Honor of the 75th Anniversary of the University of Rochester's Institute of Optics edited by Carlos R. Stroud Jr. (2004)

It'll Ease the Pain: Poems and Stories by Frank J. Edwards (2004)

For The Enrichment of Community Life: George Eastman and the Founding of the Eastman School of Music by Vincent A. Lenti (2004)

Compeer: Recovery Through the Healing Power of Friends edited by Bernice W. Skirboll with Lois Bennett and Mark Klemens (2006)

Serving a Great and Nobel Art: Howard Hanson and the Eastman School of Music by Vincent A. Lenti (2009)

Leading the Way: Eastman and Oral Health by Elizabeth Brayer (2009), recounting the history of the Eastman Dental Center

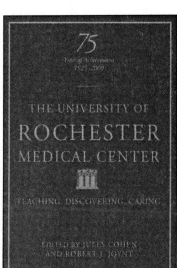

75
Years of Achievement
1925–2000

THE UNIVERSITY OF
ROCHESTER
MEDICAL CENTER

TEACHING, DISCOVERING, CARING

EDITED BY JULES COHEN
AND ROBERT J. JOYNT

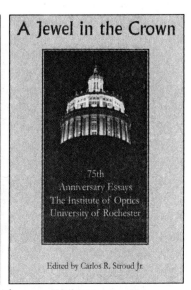

A Jewel in the Crown

75th
Anniversary Essays
The Institute of Optics
University of Rochester

Edited by Carlos R. Stroud Jr.

FOR THE ENRICHMENT
OF COMMUNITY LIFE

George Eastman and the Founding
of the Eastman School of Music

VINCENT A. LENTI

SERVING A GREAT AND NOBLE ART
Howard Hanson and the Eastman School of Music

Vincent A. Lenti

chapter 7

COOPERATIVE VENTURES

Proceedings in Long Parliament

THE YALE CENTER FOR PARLIAMENTARY HISTORY (YCPH) brought its series of editions of parliamentary proceedings to the University of Rochester Press in 1997. This series has served as a significant primary resource for parliamentary historians and historians of England in the seventeenth century for the past thirty years. Work leading to this series began in the 1930s, was interrupted by World War II, and resumed in 1965 with support from the newly instituted National Endowment for the Humanities. In the late 1970s, Yale University Press began the publication of the multi-volume proceedings in the parliament of 1628. It subsequently printed editions of the proceedings from 1625 and 1626.

In 1996 David Underdown, then director of the YCPH, and Maija Jansson, executive editor, approached the University of Rochester Press about moving the series from Yale to Rochester, hoping to increase marketing exposure beyond the United States through a global marketing program for the series; the University of Rochester Press was therefore attractive because of its international distribution arrangement with Boydell & Brewer. The staff and boards of the YCPH were pleased to have URP take over publication of the series. David Underdown retired from the directorship and Maija Jansson has continued as both director and executive editor.

The back stock for all previous volumes was transferred to the University of Rochester Press from Yale in 1997. YCPH initially contracted with URP for the publication of a four-volume edition of Proceedings in the Opening Session of the Long Parliament in the Lower House. After work began, however, it became clear that the materials would not fit in four volumes and ultimately the series swelled to seven volumes. The last volume was published in 2007.

These publications of proceedings in the early Stuart parliaments provide scholars with as full an account of what was said in a given session of parliament as is possible to reconstruct. And they provide the only complete modern texts of the diaries and notes taken by MPs. As early as 1626 it was decided by members of parliament that speeches given on the House floor or in committee meetings were not to be included in the Journals of the House of Commons for fear they might incriminate members. If the Crown chose to disregard the privileges of members to speak freely in the House, those members could be held accountable and the speech copied into the Journal would serve to convict them. These editions are the records of the parliaments that bore witness to the struggle to set limits on the power of the throne and, in so doing, they laid the foundation of modern representative democracy.

In a ceremony in the State Rooms of the Speaker's House in parliament in March 2006 Richard C. Levin, president of Yale University, presented Moroccan-bound, gold

Presentation of *Proceedings and Debates of the English Parliaments from 1625 to 1641* to the English House of Commons

stamped volumes of the editions of Proceedings and Debates of the English Parliaments from 1625 to 1641 to the English House of Commons.

In the absence of a permanent endowment, however, and without long-term funding, the Yale Center for Parliamentary History closed after the publication of the last volume on the opening session of the Long Parliament. The YCPH library has become part of the Yale British Studies initiative at Yale. Moreover, students who wish to continue to research the work of the early Stuart parliaments will soon be able to do so using not only the library but also materials online. As this brief account is being written, funding is being sought for a collaborative project between Yale University and British History Online to digitize all of the parliamentary proceedings and make them available globally at no cost.

Studies in Comparative History

The Shelby Cullom Davis Center for Historical Research at Princeton University

For more than thirty years, the Shelby Cullom Davis Center for Historical Research, founded by Lawrence Stone in 1968, has invited scholars from around the world to spend a semester or a year at Princeton University. The scholars meet once a week in a seminar and spend the rest of their time pursuing their own research. A common theme is chosen by a committee of Princeton history department members, who participate in the seminars by sharing their own work. A theme is assigned to the series of seminars, changing every two years; the Davis Center then gathers into volumes select papers on each theme.

In November of 2001, Anthony Grafton, director of the Davis Center, approached the University of Rochester Press about publishing these volumes in a series titled Studies in Comparative History. At the time, the Davis Center had five volumes in various stages of preparation. The Press and Center worked out a contractual agreement that remained in effect until 2007; over the six-year relationship, the Press published seven titles in the Davis Center series.

Titles in the series included *Animals in Human Histories: The Mirror of Nature and Culture,* edited by Mary Henninger-Voss; *The Animal/Human Boundary: Historical Perspectives,* edited by Angela N. H. Creager and William Chester Jordan; *Conversion: Old Worlds and New* and *Conversion in Late Antiquity and the Early Middle Ages: Seeing and Believing,* both edited by Kenneth Mills and Anthony Grafton; *Corrupt Histories,* edited by Emmanuel Kreike and

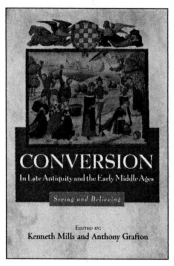

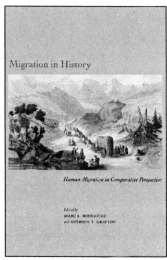

William Chester Jordan; *Repositioning North American Migration History: New Directions in Modern Continental Migration, Citizenship, and Community,* edited by Marc S. Rodriguez; *Migration in History: Human Migration in Comparative Perspective* edited by Marc S. Rodriguez and Anthony T. Grafton; and *The Nature of Cities: Culture, Landscape, and Urban Space,* edited by Andrew C. Isenberg.

According to Gyan Prakash, Grafton's predecessor at the Davis Center, "we have found Rochester superbly professional and efficient . . . the volumes have come out expeditiously and the Press has been very helpful and cooperative." In 2006, the director of Princeton University Press approached Prakash about publishing the Davis Center volumes and co-sponsoring and co-funding its Lawrence Stone Lecture Series. The Davis Center committee agreed to pursue this opportunity with its home press, and the

Davis Center concluded its publication agreements with the University of Rochester Press in September of 2006 (with the final URP-produced volume releasing in 2007).

The North American Kant Society

This series consists of a succession of volumes, chosen primarily for their interest to the members of the North American Kant Society. The membership of the society, founded in 1985 by Hoke Robinson, includes academic scholars throughout North America with a primary or secondary interest in the philosophy of Immanuel Kant. Kant's work covers a wide variety of topics including epistemology, metaphysics, ethics, politics, aesthetics, law, and religion.

Treatment of these topics may take the form of an original monograph, essay collection, translation, reprint, or bibliography. The series was originally published by Ridgeview Publishing Company, which produced the first five volumes.

The University of Rochester Press assumed responsibility for publishing the series in 2001, and to date has published three volumes including *Selected Essays on Kant by Lewis White Beck,* edited by Hoke Robinson. The late Lewis White Beck was a distinguished professor at the University of Rochester for many years. The book of essays was first printed in 2002 and reprinted in 2004. *Kantian Virtue at the Intersection of Politics and Nature: The Vale of Soul-Making,* by Scott M. Roulier, was published in 2004 and received the following praise from *German Studies Review:* "This is a valuable book for seminars in philosophy, political science, ethics, law, and environmental science." The latest book, *Understanding Purpose: Kant and the Philosophy of Biology,* edited by Philippe Huneman, was published in 2007.

LOOKING FORWARD

B Y REMAINING SMALL, AGILE, AND FOCUSED, the University of Rochester Press has flourished during twenty years of arguably the most turbulent period in the history of liberal arts publishing. It has established itself as a publisher of choice for authors generating work in its key subject areas at a time when few university presses are able to undertake the risk of publishing highly specialized books for limited audiences. Moreover, by embracing a philosophy of innovation and cautious growth, the Press has entered the twenty-first century well positioned to respond to rapid and sometimes radical changes to scholarly communications and to the dissemination of research. With the proliferation and ready availability of e-books, Google's massive efforts to digitize the contents of major U.S. research libraries, and seismic changes to the delivery of scholarly research as predicted by Open Access advocates, the University of Rochester Press will continue to monitor and respond to the needs and preferences of its readers in the academic community and beyond.

The Press in its practices and publishing program continues to be strongly editorially driven and conscious of its role in serving and representing the University of

Rochester. In so doing it aligns itself with the University's commitment to academic excellence and furthering its reputation as a top-rated private research institution. In its twentieth year, the Press has effectively fortified its established series in music history, African studies, medical history, early modern European history, and Central and Eastern European studies. Its list will continue to grow in these areas, and new and related series reflecting topical links to the University of Rochester's academic programs and areas of growth will be launched.

In recognizing that university presses have a responsibility to preserve the history, customs, and culture of the regions in which they operate, the Press's strategic plan for editorial growth includes a commitment to increasing regional publishing activity and partnering with community organizations on general-interest publications to showcase the historical and cultural treasures of western New York State. And through its Meliora imprint, the Press will continue to work collaboratively with faculty, staff, and alumni to publish thoughtfully designed books of special interest to the University of Rochester community.

In response to the need for reasonably priced books suitable for course adoption, the Press has instituted an active paperback reprint program using print-on-demand (POD) technology. This same technology also allows the Press to keep older books in print indefinitely—even as demand for those titles inevitably slows over time—and permits a reduction of (otherwise prohibitive) printing and warehousing costs. With the help of staff in the Woodbridge, England, office of Boydell & Brewer, the University of Rochester Press now makes its complete backlist available in e-book form through aggregators such as NetLibrary,

MyiLibrary, eBrary, and DawsonEra. A new Press website responds to the sharply growing use of the Internet to find, browse, and order books, and includes author tools to aid in manuscript preparation. These are, of course, only prelude to the dramatic changes in digital format and dissemination that will transform the work of all scholarly presses in the years ahead.

The unique partnership between the University and an independent scholarly publisher that enabled the creation of the Press twenty years ago also presents a collaborative, sustainable model for scholarly press operations in a new age. Sales of the Press's books have provided an ongoing income stream to the University, while production, sales, and marketing support from Boydell & Brewer minimizes the University's financial risk. All University of Rochester Press books are released simultaneously in the U.S. and in the U.K., and are promoted, sold, and distributed internationally from the first print run, a great benefit to its authors.

Operating under the auspices of the University provost's office, the Press, in addition to disseminating the fruits of faculty work, takes seriously its role as a resource for the University community. Press staff members welcome questions from and consultations with University faculty members about preparing and submitting book proposals, negotiating contract terms, and the specifics of the book production process. The Press has long published exceptional work from younger scholars in select fields, and can therefore offer editorial guidance to early-career University faculty readying their work for publication with a university or commercial scholarly press.

Libraries play a significant part not only in archiving scholarly work, but increasingly in providing equitable access to that work. The Press is fortunate to have a collegial relationship with the University's innovative River Campus Libraries and will follow closely developments in digital access and information delivery led by the libraries' staff.

In the midst of change, the Press will continue to maintain its stringent peer review procedures, underscoring the real value university presses bring to publishing: the certification of new scholarship. As delivery methods become decoupled from editorial review and quality assurance in an effort to improve accessibility, the role of publishers will shift, the responsibility for editorial control will become more diffuse, and financial models will become more complicated. Ever entrepreneurial, the University of Rochester Press will adapt and meet the challenges of a new era in scholarly communication by remaining close to its original purpose: contributing to the scholarly dialogue nationally and internationally in the University of Rochester's areas of strength.

∽ APPENDIX

University of Rochester Press

Suzanne E. Guiod, Editorial Director

Editorial Board

Editorial Advisory Board

Stanley Engerman, John Munro Professor of Economics, Professor of Economics and of History

Susan Gibbons, Vice Provost and Andrew H. & Janet Dayton Neilly Dean River Campus Libraries

Stephen J. Kunitz, MD, Professor Emeritus of Community and Preventive Medicine

Elizabeth West Marvin, Professor of Music Theory